ROOTED
IN DESIGN

THE TIME-LIFE
ENCYCLOPEDIA
OF GARDENING

Trees

THE TIME-LIFE
ENCYCLOPEDIA
OF GARDENING

Foliage House Plants

THE TIME-LIFE
ENCYCLOPEDIA
OF GARDENING

Winter Garden

THE TIME-LIFE
ENCYCLOPEDIA
OF GARDENING

Evergreens

THE TIME-LIFE
ENCYCLOPEDIA
OF GARDENING

Garden Construction

ROOTED IN DESIGN

Sprout Home's Guide to Creative Indoor Planting

Tara Heibel & Tassy de Give

PHOTOS BY
Ramsay de Give & Maria Lawson

TEN SPEED PRESS
Berkeley

INTRODUCTION

Lush, living greenery is undoubtedly beneficial to so many aspects of our lives. Surrounding ourselves with it connects the city dweller to the natural world and reminds us that we have a symbiotic relationship. A room filled with plants can be calming and inspirational as well as incredibly personal and expressive. Each plant has its own character and can speak volumes if given a platform. Even aloe, a common household plant, can exude complexity and style when displayed creatively. It was this basic connection with plants that germinated Sprout Home, a business that started as a seed in our heads and grew to what it is today.

Sprout Home is built upon the talent and knowledge of many gardeners and designers, but the two of us, Tara Heibel and Tassy de Give, head its crew and community. Tara got her start with plants by designing and planting gardens in rehabbed homes throughout Chicago's eclectic West Town neighborhood. Plant addiction took hold and a business venture turned into a passion and a lifestyle. In 2003, she founded Sprout Home's Chicago store, where she hired Tassy as her very first employee. After four years of shadowing Tara, Tassy moved to New York to open the Brooklyn location. So that's us! Basically, we're two plant lovers who hang out with plants like they're people and we're in the business of sharing that feeling!

We opened Sprout Home to be a modern home and garden center as well as a think tank for bringing plant life and good design into the homes and work spaces of beginning gardeners and experienced plant aficionados alike. Our objectives have remained the same from day one: to provide artful education to the public, to source practical and well-designed gardening products, and to bring more diverse plant options to our growing community of gardeners and plant enthusiasts.

This work never gets old, and we still act like children on Christmas Day when we receive our weekly plant deliveries. Sometimes we come across a new species that we've never seen before. Other times an old favorite is suddenly blooming. It's this love for the unexpected and appreciation for the marvels of nature that is at the root of our passion for plants.

As serious plant admirers, we thrive on introducing people to plants they've never seen. For instance, have you seen the undeniably striking and colorful leaves of Rex begonias? How about the beadlike flowers of some *Hoya*, which look like upside-down chandeliers? Recently, all of us at Sprout Home have fallen for the gold-tipped flowers of *Syngonanthus chrysanthus* 'Mikado'—a plant straight out of a sci-fi movie—and we have been thrilled to watch customers' astonished response to its fauxhawk foliage.

For anyone without a yard or other outdoor space, indoor plants are a way to stay connected to nature. And even if you do have access to public gardens and parks, living with indoor plants is a way to create a more calming and natural environment in your home. Whether your indoor garden is planted where you live or where you work, plants can be beneficial to your mind-set, health, and overall well-being. This book focuses on the joy of choosing, caring for, and displaying indoor plants, while guiding you through some of their challenges so you can delight in all the benefits indoor gardening offers.

Having been open for more than a decade, Sprout Home has given us the opportunity to listen to the difficulties our customers face in their horticultural endeavors. Most of the questions we get fall into four basic topics: How do I know which plant to select? How do I care for it? What type of container should I use? Where am I going to display it? Whether you're a notorious plant killer or a houseplant authority, the many possible answers to these simple questions can sometimes feel overwhelming. In this book, we'll talk about what it means to be a "plant parent" so that you can make smart choices about which plants do best for your environment.

PLANTS SHOWN FROM LEFT: DESERT TERRARIUM, *CRASSULA OVATA*

PLANT SHOWN: DRIED AMARANTHUS

While we love the textures, colors, and forms of plants themselves, we also consider their context. How are plants utilized in a living or workspace? How will the plant complement the style of its surroundings? Many homes and offices have design obstacles and construction restrictions, such as high windows or ledges, small rooms, and impractical layouts. When you're faced with these obstacles, the solutions are not always obvious, but they can sometimes lead to unexpected and quite beautiful results. If your home lacks floor space, consider looking up to find other areas for display. All rooms have walls and ceilings. Why not use them? The small windowsill that you thought needed a little greenery can be turned into a kitchen garden. The bare white wall that you're not allowed to paint can be trained with climbing vines that provide some natural color. We hope the plants and planting designs in this book will pleasantly surprise you as well as help you realize how many options you do have as an indoor gardener.

Our goal with this book is to provide guidance on modern indoor plant design in a straightforward and accessible way. We have documented a wide variety of stylish spaces to use as inspiration for your own site-specific plant installations. Our step-by-step instructions will help you create some of the beautiful projects we've featured. Finally, we've gathered up our best advice to help you care for your plants, which you'll find starting on page 181. With these tools at your fingertips and the know-how to push the design envelope, you will be well on your way to adding some lasting beauty to your everyday surroundings. Now, grab your gloves and let's get started!

TARA HEIBEL & TASSY DE GIVE

Look around your space. Is there a wall that always looks empty? An awkward spot that you don't know what to do with but is begging for some attention? You might have thought about displaying artwork, but why not use plants instead? In urban living environments where horizontal real estate is limited, wall plantings free up valuable tabletop and floor space, and also keep flora away from children and pets. "Planting" your walls instead of your floors or tabletops treats your greenery like the art that it is.

1: ON THE WALL

PLANTING ON A WALL CAN BE CHALLENGING, so you'll need to think about some logistics before you begin. Pay attention to the light that's in the area. How many hours of light does your target area receive? What is the quality of that light? How easy will it be to water the plants there? How much clearance will you need for the plants to protrude from the wall without inhibiting walkways?

Just as different styles of art can create different moods, the types of plants used in a wall planting can dictate the experience that the viewer will have. A diverse palette of color and texture creates a dynamic, eye-catching display, while a monotone, low-profile approach using the same plants or soft colors creates a calming atmosphere. After considering your plant palette, think about how you would like to arrange the plants in terms of size and scale. When utilizing smaller objects as planters, keep in mind the viewer's eye level and how the installation will be viewed. Are you looking for an understated natural style with a simple vase of leaves, or do you need something more dramatic like covering the entire wall with moss? Pay attention to how large the wall is as well as the objects around it. Is it large enough for multiple mountings or would a minimalist approach be best? If there is already a lot going on in the space, you might want to use one large planting, but if your goal is to break up a monotonous space, then several plantings might add intrigue.

After considering plant choices and arrangement, think about the mechanics of mounting your hanging garden. Of course, you could have custom wall systems built to fit your specifications, but for most of us, this is not financially realistic. Fortunately, there are other options for creating pieces of living wall art that are much more cost-effective and easy to maintain.

If you are purchasing a prebuilt system and planning on using it inside, first verify that it is intended for indoor use and that it will not water your walls as well as your plants! With most prebuilt systems, the plants will be in one container and in the same soil. So, make sure that the plants play nicely together—in other words, if all the plants are in the same planter, they should be plants that share the same soil, water, and light requirements.

When selecting plants for a group container, think about how each one will grow and imagine what they will look like in a few months or even in a few years. Consider their shape, size, and texture. Keep in mind that the plants you see at your local garden center might be young and immature, so you should inquire as to how they will fill out over time. Some customers are surprised when they learn the difference in appearance between a young plant and a mature plant. With a little bit of preparation and inspiration from the projects that follow, you can create custom wall plantings that will enliven your indoor space and show off plants in an unexpected way.

PLANTS SHOWN: *SEDUM, DYCKIA, CRASSULA, CRYPTANTHUS, ECHEVERIA*

CLEAR VASES FOR
PLANT CUTTINGS

One of the easiest ways to incorporate greenery into your home without committing to taking care of a plant is by using cuttings—pieces of plants that have been separated from the parent and displayed in glass vessels. Cuttings can last for months and give you the flexibility to change the design on your wall on a whim. They are easy to set up and require minimal maintenance, making them perfect for the novice indoor gardener. Designing with plant cuttings also allows you to expand your plant collection via propagation. Utilizing clear glass vessels to house your cuttings, you can witness one of the most intriguing aspects of propagation by watching the development of the root system.

Ideally, you want to find vases that have a hole for hanging them already in the glass so that mounting them is as simple as putting a nail or screw in the wall. If you are unable to source vessels with premade holes, try containers that have a lip or grooves at the top, such as mason jars, that you can wrap a piece of wire or string around. After you've wrapped the wire or string around the vase, make a small loop that can be used to hang the vessel on a nail or screw inserted in the wall. We recommend using simply shaped vessels in order to highlight the plant material. If you would like to draw more attention to the vase itself, consider using small rocks or other decorative material at the bottom of the vases to add more interest to the presentation.

To make a cutting, prune a plant just below the node of a stem or cut the entire stem of the plant. Remove any leaves from the stem that will be below the water line, as submerged leaves will cause the water to grow bacteria, which may kill the cutting. Fill the vase with room-temperature water.

Maintenance for cutting vases is easy: Keep the water level full and change the water whenever it gets cloudy. Part sun is best for plant cuttings. It's also a good idea to fertilize the cutting once a month by adding a few drops of liquid fertilizer to the vase water. When the cutting's roots have filled the container (in about one to six months), you can plant the cutting in soil and begin another.

Most cuttings will begin to root between seven to twenty-one days. It's important to keep in mind that not all cuttings will root, so don't get discouraged if you don't see any roots growing. Just prune off any brown or yellow leaves. This will give more energy to developing new growth. Some plants that work well for cutting vases are *Begonia rex, Chlorophytum, Dracaena, Epipremnum, Ficus, Gynura, Hedera helix, Philodendron, Schefflera, Yucca,* and *Zamioculcas zamiifolia.*

PLANTS SHOWN OPPOSITE FROM LEFT: *MONSTERA DELICIOSA, HEDERA HELIX, ZAMIOCULCAS ZAMIIFOLIA, BEGONIA REX, EPIPREMNUM PICTUM*

MASON JAR WALL PLANTERS

Mason jars are classic containers that have become very popular for housing plants. They can be used individually as a vase on a tabletop or grouped together and mounted on a board for a wall display. There are pros and cons to using a mason jar as a planter. One advantage is that the clear glass allows you to see how much water and soil is in the container so that you do not overwater. A disadvantage is that the size of a mason jar is small and many plants will outgrow the container and need repotting sooner rather than later. As long as you select plants that can withstand minimal watering and grow slowly, mason jars are a charming and affordable option for a wall-mounted planter. We favor preassembled mason jar wall planters—they usually come with three jars per arrangement, with hinges that allow you to remove the jars for easy maintenance. (You can always make your own as well with a simple trip to the hardware store to source the components. Weight is a consideration with board-mounted pieces, so be sure to use the appropriate anchors.)

A mason jar doesn't have a hole for drainage, so create faux drainage by placing a one-inch layer of small rocks on the bottom of the container below the soil. The rocks will help keep excess water from the plant's roots. A good option is small lava rocks because they are lightweight and porous. Water each plant with about one cup of water per jar. The soil should be slightly dry to the touch before you water the plant again.

For low to medium light spaces, consider using plants such as *Epipremnum pinnatum, Fittonia, Gynura, Hedera helix, Hypoestes, Philodendron, Pilea,* and *Zamioculcas zamiifolia.*

For high-light spaces, options include *Crassula, Echeveria, Euphorbia, Kalanchoe, Sedum, Sempervivum,* and *Senecio.*

PLANTS SHOWN OPPOSITE FROM LEFT: *FITTONIA, SOLEIROLIA SOLEIROLII, HYPOESTES*

CLIMBING VINES

Indoor vines can be used to create the illusion that nature has crept into your home. Most vines are fast growers and have a meandering shape to them that stands out against a wall. You can train vines to climb along a window, up a wall, or around a frame. Some will naturally cling to a wall or climb up wire supports, others will need a little help from nails or hooks. Vines are a great option to consider if you live in an apartment and are not allowed to paint, but want to add some depth, color, or texture to your walls.

Indoor vines can be divided into three primary categories: self-adhesives (suckers), support vines (tendrils and twisters), and hanging vines (leaners). Self-adhesive vines cling directly to porous surfaces via their suckers, which are roots that can bore into brick, wood, concrete, and stucco. They can be potentially harmful because they can break down the structure to which they are clinging and ruin paint. We recommend using self-adhesive vines only on a supplemental support structure that is removable, such as a trellis.

Support vines are vines that need a support system such as a trellis, wire, or stake in order to grow. They are classified as tendrils or twisters, and they attach themselves to the support either by delicate feet called tendrils or by wrapping their new growth around the support. Members of this group include *Cissus rhombifolia, Hoya, Jasminum officinale, Passiflora,* and *Thunbergia,* among others. One note of caution regarding indoor vines: Avoid placing a vine with tendrils next to a window with screens, because the tendrils may eventually tear the screen apart.

The last category of indoor vines is hanging vines, or leaners, which do not need a support structure in order to grow, but will need your help if you want to train them to grow along a wall. These vines can be attached to a wall via a "ladder" made of nails or hooks that provide them with something to lean on. Leaning vines include *Bougainvillea, Clerodendrum, Dischidia, Epipremnum pinnatum, Peperomia, Philodendron, Rhipsalis, Sedum, Senecio,* and *Tradescantia.*

You can start training indoor vines when they are young or when an older plant sends out long trailers. For young vines, set up a system using fishing line or wire for the vine to grab onto and grow. As the vine develops, wrap the leaves around the line (sometimes the vine will do it naturally). Then you just need a little time and patience while the vine does most of the work for you. With established longer vines you can use finishing nails to act as anchors for the leaves and map out a path in whatever configuration you'd like. Finishing nails have a small head and diameter that makes them great to use when you want the nail to be hidden. The instant gratification of a longer vine really allows you to play with direction and shape. Most vines grow to a length of five to twenty-five feet. In the project shown opposite, *Philodendron* 'Brazil' vines were attached to the walls in a bedroom. Finishing nails were used to make a ladder, and the leaves were placed over the nails to provide them with something to hang on. If you have a large wall, use multiple plants in opposite corners in order to allow for the vines to expand in different directions. Once the vines grow to your desired length, simply prune back any growth to keep your design maintained.

PLANT SHOWN OPPOSITE: *PHILODENDRON* 'BRAZIL'

WALL BRICKS

Sometimes a wall would benefit not only from plants, but also from a bold color statement. One way to incorporate a shot of color is to use vibrant plant containers. The manner in which you arrange the planters can also add texture and depth to a room. If your room has a long horizontal wall, you can play on this by giving more space in between each container, emphasizing the wall's length. If you have a vertical space to work with, or are uncertain about what style might work, try a staggered formation from floor to ceiling; it rarely works to your disadvantage.

In the installation above, the ceramic bricks are configured according to color and placed on the wall in a staggered formation. You could also use multiple containers that are the same color in order to keep the design more neutral. Use containers that have the same color tone—for example, all pastels or all bold colors. Also, think about how the color is going to play off of the other items in your space, such as the walls, furniture, and accessories. Do you want the boldest item in the room to be the color of the wall planters, or would you prefer the wall garden to be more subtle?

When you're using wall-mounted containers such as the ones shown opposite, choose slow-growing plants that have shallow root systems, and choose the same type of plant for each container—for example, all succulents or all ferns. Using the same type of plants with the same water and light needs will make caring for them easier. Succulents are used here because they have shallow roots. You could also use *Begonia, Fittonia, Peperomia, Philodendron,* or *Pilea* for a low-light option.

Once you have chosen the plants, you can focus on the layout of the containers. Experiment with different combinations before actually planting to determine which arrangement you like best. Try mixing trailing plants with upright ones to create variation in form. Use texture and color to create contrast and distinction. The dusty purple flowerlike leaves of an *Echeveria* 'Perle von Nürnberg' can prove to be a striking contrast to a cascading *Sedum* or *Crassula.* Remember to think about how each plant will grow and what you want the focal point to be. If you have gaps in between the plants and want a fuller look, you can place bits of preserved reindeer moss in your planting. Gold reindeer moss was used in the project opposite and provides a nice contrast to the blue wall and neutral-colored planters.

Next, don't forget that the plants will need proper drainage. If the vessel does not have a drain hole, create drainage by placing a layer of rocks (we recommend small lava rocks) in the base of the container. Be careful when watering to ensure you do not water your wall as well as your plants. You may want to use a shot glass to water each plant or a watering can with a thin nozzle to control the flow and ensure you do not overwater.

PLANTS SHOWN OPPOSITE: *CRASSULA, ECHEVERIA, SEDUM*

LIGHT AND AIRY

If your wall space is limited but you still want to install something decorative on it, the simple architectural form and variety of *Tillandsia,* or air plants, may fit the bill. These plants do not require soil to grow, so they are simple to mount on walls.

For this arrangement, prism-shaped metal frames were wired together to create a three-dimensional sculpture. The wire forms are so light that only very simple supports, such as small nails or no-tear hanging hooks, were needed. Dried and preserved reindeer moss was used to visually ground the air plants, making them look as if they are growing from a base or medium (although air plants don't need a medium in which to grow).

If you want a stronger visual statement on your wall, use pigment-concentrated preserved moss and opaque vessels in a similar arrangement as the wire forms. Plan the arrangement carefully so that the display will be harmonious and balanced. Even if you want the configuration to appear randomly arranged, it should still be controlled chaos. The *Tillandsia* specimens can be rotated, creating an ever-changing piece of art for your wall. If you're using reindeer moss, be careful not to allow the reindeer moss to become saturated with water—some of the color preservatives could transfer to the wall's surface and possibly stain it. From a dense composition to a minimalist arrangement, the direction this installation takes is up to you!

PLANTS SHOWN OPPOSITE: MIXED *TILLANDSIA*

WALL PLANTERS

One of the best ways to prevent pets from nibbling on your plants is to elevate them. This can be done with any sort of pocket planter, such as the plywood accordion planters pictured here, but there are dozens of types available to fit your individual style. Placing the planters in a group can also create a nice focal point for a room. In the example above, one of these wall planters is being used as a bookshelf while the others contain foliage that make the room all the more interesting.

For wall containers, think of the effect you want the finished planting to achieve. How do you want to draw the eye through the room? Plants that grow vertically will draw the eye upward and also potentially save some valuable walking space below. Do you have high ceilings, and wall space that allows for higher vessel placement? If so, you may want to consider a selection of cascading plants with a downward vining growth habit to create intimacy.

The various dimensions and textures of the plants you select will create a mood for your space. Do you want your space to feel soft, warm, and cozy, or bold, structured, and crisp? Remember to choose plant groupings that share similar care preferences if you are planting them in the same container.

And again, consider drainage and how it will affect how much water you supply the plants. If you're using permeable planters, line them with waterproof material and conduct a water test with the vessel before installing it to see if any water leaks through—leaking water might damage your wall.

For walls that receive full sun, consider desert plants such as *Crassula*, *Echeveria*, *Sedum*, *Sempervivum*, or *Senecio*. For low to medium sunlight, a combination of *Asparagus densiflorus*, *Chlorophytum*, *Epipremnum pinnatum*, *Hedera helix*, *Philodendron*, or *Tradescantia* are good options. Remember to keep the location of your wall planter in mind. For plants that require more water, accessibility is key. Succulents require less water and can therefore be placed in a higher location, provided they have adequate sunlight.

The single plantings shown opposite demonstrate potential colors and texture combinations. The pockets themselves are neutral, so the leaves of *Begonia rex* and finely textured ferns such as the *Athyrium* lady fern create contrast and complement the container. If you'd prefer to see less of the container and more of the plants, include more trailing plants. Conversely, if you'd like to bring more attention to the vessel itself and create a more cohesive and uniform look, use the same plant in each container. Planting in multiples of the same plant allows the viewer's eye to rest and focus in on the design details of the plants and the repetition of containers.

PLANTS SHOWN OPPOSITE FROM LEFT: *BEGONIA REX*, FERN

Pockets composed of breathable felt and an interior recycled plastic liner are another option for wall planters. In the example shown opposite, the project is planted with desert plants. Because these plants like to dry out in between watering, they are a good option for such a precarious position—you won't need to climb up there and water them very often. The vertical nature of the *Aloe* plant pictured here and the skeletal structure of the *Euphorbia milii* give the planting its height. The *Rhipsalis*, *Hoya*, and hanging *Sedum* fill in the midsection as they cascade downward. Velvety, dried *Amaranthus* drips from each pocket, adding additional interest. Not all of your plants have to be living. Dried plants add excellent textural interest. The *Amaranthus* is preserved, so it can be moved around as the live plants fill in over time.

PLANTS SHOWN OPPOSITE: *EUPHORBIA MILII, RHIPSALIS, HOYA, SEDUM, ALOE, DRIED AMARANTHUS*

THE RECYCLED WALL

When you're considering vessels to house your plants on your walls, use your creativity and think about transforming found objects into planters. Wood pallets, old tires, soda bottles, and tin cans can all be retrofitted for housing plants on a wall. Above is the DesignProject Meter Box, or DP1 wall terrarium, a repurposed electric meter box. The wall terrarium can be mounted via the original back plates, but if your found object does not already have a hanging mechanism, use French cleats or picture-hanging hardware. Whatever hanging mechanism is used, make sure it allows for easy removal from the wall so that the vessel can be watered. The product designer of the DP1 terrarium added a half wall made of acrylic at the back of the terrarium to keep the soil in place, and since the acrylic is clear you can see what is happening in the bottom layers from the back side as well.

The DP1 wall meters are a good example of how using multiples of the same vessel makes a strong impact on a large wall. Succulents were used in these plantings because they have a shallow root system and can be planted together without requiring a lot of space. If your wall does not receive direct sun, use succulents that are tolerant of bright filtered light, such as *Aloe*, *Crassula*, *Haworthia*, and *Rhipsalis*.

You can also add interest to this planting using layers of colored sand or decorative rocks for contrasting layers or visual pop at the soil line. Make sure the decorative layers reach the glass, because you'll only be able to see the layers that are in direct contact with the glass. And, as with any type of container that does not have a drain hole, you'll need to create a drainage layer using rocks.

Care for meter terrariums is easy. Before doing any watering, let your newly potted succulents settle in for seven to ten days. This will help their delicate roots adjust to the new planting. Then give each plant approximately one shot glass of water. Wait until the soil feels dry near the base of each plant before you water again. These plants require direct light for optimal health. Even though there is a vent at the top of each meter, the humidity conserved in such a vessel will help water the plant.

Although we recommend shallow-rooted succulents for the DP1 wall terrariums, there are other plants that would also work well in them. In a space with filtered light, use live moss or ground cover such as *Pilea depressa*, *Soleirolia soleirolii*, *Ficus pumila*, and *Muehlenbeckia axillaris*.

PLANTS SHOWN BELOW: MIXED SUCCULENTS

MOUNTED CONSTRUCTIONS

Perhaps you have a sublet that you want to spruce up quickly without investing a lot of time and money. This is an occasion where epiphytic plants are an excellent option. A quick review for us non-rain-forest natives: An epiphyte is a plant that anchors on another plant (called a host plant) or object and gets its nutrition and water from the debris and moisture in the air. In other words, it does not need soil to grow. Epiphytic plants can be found in temperate and tropic zones worldwide, and can include *Tillandsia*, mosses, ferns, orchids, bromeliads, and even some cacti.

Mounting an epiphyte is easy. All you need are some basic materials: the plants and the surface on which you are going to mount them. Before you begin, make sure your wall has adequate natural light for the plants you've selected. Then choose the wood or other material you'll be using. Consider using found or salvaged materials. Driftwood and reclaimed pieces add an additional level of visual interest to the mount. Just make sure any wood you use can withstand getting wet without rotting, such as cedar or teak. Also, you must be able to drill into the mounting surface in order to install it on the wall.

Consider how you are going to affix your installation to a wall. Whether you're using wire-hanging screws, eye hooks, or another mechanism, use at least two anchor points so that the installation is secure. One point of contact will most likely not be strong enough to hold the weight of a mounted plant, especially if it's large.

Did you know that one-third of ferns are actually epiphytic and can be mounted? One of our favorite epiphytic plants to use for this type of installation is *Platycerium bifurcatum* or *Platycerium superbum*, aka staghorn ferns (see page 28). The staghorn fern is sculptural in form and quite unusual—it actually has two sets of leaves: a sterile set and a fertile set. The sterile leaves—known as the mantle or basal plate—are flat, shieldlike, and turn brown periodically. The fertile leaves are green and have an unmistakable form, which earns the fern its nickname. When working with staghorn ferns, be careful not to harm or remove the sterile leaves; while they may have a messy appearance, removing them can harm the plant.

PLANTS SHOWN OPPOSITE FROM LEFT: MOUNTED *PLATYCERIUM*, *BEGONIA ACONITIFOLIA*

MAKE
YOUR
OWN

MOUNTED STAGHORN FERN

MATERIALS

French cleats or other
hanging mechanism
to hang the board

Sphagnum moss

Bucket

4 screws or nails
(with heads that are
large enough for
wire to be secured
around them)

Screwdriver or hammer

Wood board
(the board used here
is 16" x 16"; select a
board that is at least
20 percent larger than
the grower's pot your
plant came in to allow
for future growth)

6" staghorn fern

Fishing wire
or coated wire

STEP 1 Using French cleats or another type of hanging hardware, affix a hanging mechanism to the back of your board.

STEP 2 Soak the sphagnum moss in a bucket of water until it's fully saturated. Remove the moss and wring it out so that it is not dripping prior to use.

STEP 3 Secure the screws about 2 inches away from where you are going to place the sterile leaves* of the staghorn fern. This spacing will allow room for new growth. Leave a small bit of space at the top so you can wind wire around them.

STEP 4 On the board, lay most of the damp sphagnum moss in the middle of the screws (reserve some for use in step 7). Arrange the moss in a bed that is a little more shallow in the middle and a little bit bulkier around the edges.

STEP 5 Remove the fern from its pot and carefully remove all of the soil from its roots.

STEP 6 Spread the roots gently into the middle of the sphagnum moss, paying attention to the direction and form of the leaves and how they will look when the board is displayed on a wall. From what angle will you view the mounting? Make sure that the plant is showing its good side.

STEP 7 Once the fern is in place, pack a little more of the sphagnum moss around its base to cover the rest of the root system, but be sure not to cover the fern's sterile leaves.

STEP 8 Secure the fern to the board using clear fishing line or coated wire. You can use any kind of material that blends in as long as it will not deteriorate. Tie the line to one of the screws and then draw the line in a crisscross pattern across the sphagnum moss from screw to screw to secure the fern and the moss in place. Once the fern is completely secure, tie the end of the line around another screw.

*NOTE: STERILE LEAVES ARE FLAT, SHIELDLIKE, AND TURN BROWN PERIODICALLY.

For more on how to care for this project, see page 208.

FAUX LIVING WALL

At Sprout Home, we get a lot of requests from customers who want to install a living moss wall in their home. Because moss likes to be consistently moist at all times, it is very hard to keep it alive in a home environment. You would need to create a frame that would not only protect your walls, but hold the moss structure as well. For most homes, whether they're apartments or houses, it's not feasible to do this successfully.

However, there is a way to create the same aesthetic resonance using dried moss. Creating a dried moss arrangement is all about combining various textures and colors to mimic a landscape. A variety of dried and preserved moss (which is simply moss that has been treated to enhance its color) is available at most garden centers and craft stores. A good selection for natural-looking carpet moss is mood moss or sheet moss; these can serve as the foundation for a wall planting. To create an undulating effect on your faux moss wall, use clumps of thicker dried moss with mood or sheet moss. Mixing the various types of moss, with their different proportions, creates crevices and dips on the mounted display. Use preserved reindeer moss to fill in the crevices or dips if you like, or use it for additional texture and effect.

This project is the perfect opportunity to take out that forgotten frame that has been sitting in your storage space or garage for the last few years. If the frame does not already have a back attached to it, attach one with a piece of wood cut to size and adhere it to the back of the frame with glue or nails. In addition to the frame and the dried moss, you will also need a glue gun and some sparks of creativity. The finished project has the same effect as a living moss wall, but without the maintenance. The added design elements elevate the planting to a complex and visually stunning landscape guaranteed to raise the question, "Is that real?"

PLANTS SHOWN: DRIED AND PRESERVED MOSS

MOSS WALL

MATERIALS

Screwdriver

Screws

French cleat (choose
the size appropriate for
your frame or plywood)

Frame with back
side attached to it
(or a piece of plywood
cut to whatever size
you want)

Glue cartridge

Hot-glue gun

Floral pins

1"-thick pink insulation
(available at most
hardware stores)

Mood moss

Sheet moss

Preserved reindeer
moss

Dried wood (optional):
driftwood, dried bark,
or kiwi vine

Dried floral elements
(optional): sponge
mushroom, yarrow,
Protea, or kale
(available at most craft
and floral stores)

Tillandsia specimens
(optional)

STEP 1 Using a screwdriver and screws, follow the manufacturer's instructions and attach the French cleat to the back of the frame or plywood.

STEP 2 Using a hot-glue gun and floral pins, attach the pink insulation to the front side of the frame board (or plywood).

STEP 3 Using the hot-glue gun, glue pieces of mood and sheet moss to the pink insulation to create your primary landscape. Arrange the landscape as you see fit.

STEP 4 Once the landscape base is finished, add other elements to the base. Glue bits of colored reindeer moss to the base to create additional depth.

STEP 5 If you're using dried wood or floral elements, add them to the landscape using floral pins or the hot-glue gun.

STEP 6 If you're using *Tillandsia*, add them to the landscape using floral pins or the hot-glue gun.

STEP 7 Once the glue is dry, do a wiggle test. Use your fingers to gently wiggle the elements. If they cannot be easily pulled off, they pass the test and the moss landscape is finished. Otherwise, use more glue and floral pins to secure the elements. Hang the frame.

For more on how to care for this project, see page 209.

THE BLENDED WALL

When you're designing an indoor garden, sometimes you want to emphasize the plants, and sometimes you want to emphasize the containers. The succulent wall plantings shown at left are a reinterpretation of a living wall system and create a seamless union of nature and architecture. The dark-colored containers extend from the wall, but their color blends them into the dark reclaimed wood. Each plant box tells its own story, while acting in unison on the wall. If you do not have the luxury to create a blended wall from scratch, where the containers are literally built into the wall, you can always attach containers after the fact to an existing wall. Select containers that fuse with the wall behind in color and texture. You want to mimic the setting in your home and have the containers blend in to the wall as if they do not exist. If your home is white and modern, use a basic white container; if your home has brick or weathered walls, use an aged terracotta or concrete container.

There are many different types of succulents, and most look great together. In these wall plantings, varying shades of chalk blue upright *Senecio serpens* are paired with bright green beady *Sedum* plants. The silver, star-shape leaves of a *Dyckia* play well with the scale of the planters, offering a focal point for your eye. *Euphorbia tirucalli* provides height and a threadlike texture while also adding trailing elements. There are many different types of succulents, and most look great together. When seen en masse, these box gardens create a wall of greenery that is subtle, yet beautiful and complex.

With succulents, you never know exactly what shape they're going to take when they mature. Like most plants, succulents will naturally gravitate toward the light, but as they do, they become varied in direction. That's part of their beauty, and what makes these plantings so interesting. The large skylight is ideal for succulents because they prefer bright, direct sun. All the succulents are compatible in terms of their soil moisture and watering needs.

PLANTS SHOWN OPPOSITE: MIXED SUCCULENTS

PLANT SHOWN: DYCKIA

PLANTS SHOWN: MIXED SUCCULENTS

Windowsills and ledges are where people most often place indoor plants. Although they are popular locations, these areas also pose their own set of challenges. Not only are there size constraints to be considered, but the architecture of a windowsill often has specific aesthetic needs. Think of your window frame as a painter would a canvas. Do you want your planting to be the main feature of the painting or just an accent to the view outside? There are times when location dictates that you play by its rules, such as putting succulents on a sunny window ledge, but that does not mean you cannot push the boundaries.

II: ON THE LEDGE

BEFORE PLANTING YOUR WINDOWSILL, pay attention to any mechanized parts of the window that you will need access to. Is it a window that you open and close frequently? If so, wind can become a factor, stressing plants with delicate leaf structures. Consider the amount of light that will be gracing the plants, and also the amount of light the window lets in to the room itself. In most cases, you do not want your planting to block the light coming in to your room. Also, temperatures near windows tend to fluctuate. Pay attention if a spot runs hot or cold.

How do you view the windowsill? Is it above eye level or below? Do you have one large window or multiple windows? Imagine the potential for plant growth on the windowsill and how you would prefer the plants to grow with regard to form and direction. Before you commit to a plant, ask your local garden center what the plant will look like in a year. Will it have an upright growth habit or a horizontal one? You might not want a trailing plant in an area where you'd prefer vertical growth. If your container has a drainage hole, make sure you have a saucer to put underneath it, or water the plant in a sink or bathtub. We also recommend placing a discreet piece of corkboard or a felt mat under the container(s) to help keep excess moisture from staining the windowsill.

PLANTS SHOWN OPPOSITE: *CRASSULA, ECHEVERIA*

A WORD ON BALANCE

You can use your container and plant selections to play with the proportions of a space. A window ledge is the perfect spot to do this. Place a large container to the left or right of a windowsill. Notice how it anchors the surrounding area. You can amplify this effect by placing more objects on the floor nearby. Furniture on either side of the windowsill will be part of the same frame visually. Consider it part of the larger picture.

Perhaps you have a large piece of furniture, like a solid and hefty lounge chair, that gives a heavy and weighted feeling to the room. You can use a windowsill planting to pull the eye up and out of the visual pit created by the hefty chair. Balance the visually heavy side of the room with a large container and lush plant. Choosing a plant that has broad, expansive leaves will create more of a statement. Although it might be the only planting on the windowsill, no one will miss it. Plants to consider for creating this bold statement could include various *Philodendron* varieties, larger-leaf *Ficus* such as *lyrata* or *elastica*, *Schefflera*, *Aglaonema*, and *Alocasia*. You can always pair a large plant with a smaller one to increase the close-up appeal, getting the best of both worlds: the intimate and the expansive. All on one windowsill!

PLANTS SHOWN OPPOSITE FROM LEFT: *CALADIUM, CHLOROPHYTUM, MONSTERA DELICIOSA*; BELOW: *RHIPSALIS*

PLAYING THE HIGH HORIZON

An area often overlooked for placing plants is a high ledge. The angle can be forgotten about, not thought about practically, or is just intimidating. Do not let the height of the ledge scare you, but instead take advantage of it and celebrate it! In doing so, you might want to select plants that require less watering and can handle a dry period.

A ledge can be the top of a row of wall-mounted kitchen cabinets, the deep sill of a window set high on a wall, or a second-floor walkway that's visible from the main floor. A hanging vine can be the perfect complement to help smooth over the sharp edges, create depth, and make a space seem more welcoming. If the planting becomes so gregarious that it impedes foot traffic, prune it back and shape it.

Some of our favorite trailing plants for ledges are *Philodendron friedrichsthalii*, *Philodendron scandens* or 'Brazil', *Epipremnum pinnatum*, and *Hoya*. These lush and low maintenance plants can easily hold their own both visually and practically on a ledge. Their limbs can also be trained to climb in different directions, helping to add some green to empty space on the ledge.

If you want to stretch a vine beyond the ledge, place small wall nails or hooks in the wall to support the limbs of the vine in the direction you want them to go (see page 15 for more detail). The vine may require some training, but with a little assistance it will seem natural and thoughtful.

PLANTS SHOWN OPPOSITE: *PHILODENDRON 'BRAZIL', PILEA DEPRESSA, PHILODENDRON CORDATUM, AESCHYNANTHUS*

WINDOW SEAT

Sometimes there just isn't enough space on a windowsill or ledge to place all of your sun-loving foliage. That doesn't mean you can't place your plants close to the light. A wonderful solution to this dilemma is installing a window seat. It not only serves as a sight-specific grounding surface for your foliage, but as a resting place for you.

Think of your window seat as a mini terrace, a surface that eases the transition between the softness of your plants and hardness of your interior space. We've often found these types of seats and benches serve as lookout posts, giving people an excuse to slow down and spend some time by their windows.

A window seat has the potential to serve as a unifying structure in an interior space, providing a spot for you to be closer to your greenery. Getting closer to your plants also allows you to observe and appreciate their finer features, details that you may have otherwise missed. It's always fun to rearrange and experiment with the endless possibilities of how to sit with your plants. If you have a furry little friend, don't forget to save a seat for him too.

PLANTS SHOWN ABOVE FROM LEFT: *BEGONIA, SEDUM, GASTERIA, ALOE, OPUNTIA,* GRAFTED *GYMNOCALYCIUM, KALANCHOE THYRSIFLORA;* OPPOSITE FROM LEFT: ROSEMARY, *SEDUM, CRASSULA, TILLANDSIA, BEGONIA, ALOE, ECHEVERIA*

PLANT SHOWN: *PEPEROMIA CAPERATA*

PLANTS SHOWN FROM LEFT: *MEDINILLA MAGNIFICA, GASTERIA, ALBUCA LONGIFOLIA, ECHEVERIA*

MULTIPLE CONTAINERS, ONE PLANT

It can be challenging to find just the right plants to fit on your windowsill or ledge. The normally tight proportions can be constricting, so in some cases it is best to simplify. To create a seamless look, whether you're using multiple windows or a single window, concentrate on using the same type of plant or combination of two plants to create a pattern. Repeating that pattern can visually extend the length of a space and lead the eye from one room to another while also softening any harsh lines.

Where is your ledge located? If you are viewing it straight on as you walk into a room, you will want to design it with a focal point in mind, using varying heights and containers. If it's in a hallway, you will most likely view your ledge from the side as you pass by. In this instance, take advantage of the fact that your main view is from an angle that constantly changes as you walk through the area. Creating a pattern with similar plants helps to bring your eye through the space and make it look larger than it really is. Take a walk through the area in question. Ask yourself which perspectives you'd like to highlight and accentuate, and determine the focal points.

For the hallway installation pictured opposite, we paired *Chlorophytum comosum*, which has an arching growth habit, with white containers. The plants gracefully cover the ledges while not blocking the natural light from the window. The white variegation on the plants' leaves and the white containers blend with the wall, making a seamless transition from window well to window well. This planting is easy to care for and adds just the right amount of pop to the hallway.

In spaces where there are existing long lines, reiterating that horizontal expanse with one long container might not be practical. Where on earth are you going to find a container that long? In such scenarios, we like to utilize multiple containers to create the same effect that one long container would provide. This approach breaks up long lines and encourages your eye to slow down and take in more detail. You can create container groupings or space them out, and even switch them around when you like. No matter which configuration you choose, it will still read as a singular thought and pattern.

If your ledge is already too congested and you want to create uniformity, consider using rectangular containers. Or, if more variation is needed, use rectangular containers but different types of plants. Using plants that have a vertical growth habit will contrast with the horizontal lines of the containers, and give the planting more visual impact. Plants with upright growth include *Clivia*, *Crassula*, *Croton*, *Dracaena*, *Euphorbia tirucalli*, *Sansevieria*, and *Zamioculcas zamiifolia*.

PLANTS SHOWN OPPOSITE: *CHLOROPHYTUM COMOSUM;* PLANTS SHOWN BELOW: *PLECTRANTHUS VERTICILLATUS*

MULTIPLE CONTAINERS, MULTIPLE PLANTS

Some ledges are centered in a room, where they are mostly viewed straight on, like a painting. And, like a painting, you can create your own still life by mixing and matching a selection of plants and containers. When you are grouping multiples, pay attention to how the containers relate to one another. We are not saying that everything has to match, but if the vessels do not relate to one another in any way, the grouping can appear thrown together instead of artfully arranged. Consider the color, shape, and size of the containers you're using. You can use these elements to create symmetry or to offset it. Either way, there should be some consistent element in the selection of containers so the grouping feels cohesive.

In the austere black-and-white room shown above, we gathered a collection of vintage and new pots to add color and texture to the space. Even though the shapes and styles of the containers vary, their colors have the same hue or saturation, providing some continuity for the collection. With the window framing the arrangement, it can be perceived as its own site-specific art collection, one that can be moved around and changed according to your needs or taste at any given time.

If a ledge and its surrounding area has an existing color tone, pay attention to it as you imagine the plantings you'll put there. Is it warm in nature, with hues of brown, or does it have cooler tones exhibiting hints of gray? Even neutrals have color in them. If you haven't gone shopping for paint in awhile, go to a paint store to view the options for what one would consider yellow. You'll see that the range of yellows is vast, because colors can be refined by the addition of other colors, creating ever so slight variations on the original. If you have a ledge space where there is an existing color, make sure that your planter selections complement that tone.

For the ledges below, we selected containers that vary in shape but have consistent color hues, taking our cue from the warm tones in the existing brick and wood. As a rule of thumb, when you're working with multiple pots in different shapes, use pots that have at least one consistent element among them.

Although you could use the same plant type in each of your containers, why not use this as an opportunity to vary your choices? Since each container has its own shape and personality, select plants that emphasize the aesthetics of each pot. Consider pairing vertical plants with bulbous containers, or pair plants with round leaves with square pots. Doing so reinforces the variations in form and texture, creating more complexity for the ledge planting. In the planting below, for example, the sleek *Aloe* plant echoes the smooth curves of its pot, while a *Begonia rex* leans to its side, echoing the curve of its container. Have fun with your multiple vessels and plants. With the right combination, your ledge will become a stunning framed garden.

PLANTS SHOWN OPPOSITE FROM LEFT: *SANSEVIERIA CYLINDRICA, CRASSULA COMMUTATA, ASPARAGUS DENSIFLORUS, PAPHIOPEDILUM, SELAGINELLA, HEDERA, HAWORTHIA;* BELOW FROM LEFT: *SANSEVIERIA, CRASSULA, BEGONIA REX*

Sometimes a ledge is built-in and is part of the architecture of a room. It might serve a purpose as an element of the building's framework, or it might have been added later. Regardless of why it's there, you can use it. Again, start by taking your cue from the surrounding space. For the installation below, we selected containers with rich and fully saturated hues to play off the colors in the room. The gray walls and concrete floor, along with the warm browns of the furniture and paintings, call out for a deeper, more visually grounding component. The large-leafed *Monstera deliciosa* was positioned in the corner to anchor the space and frame the paintings, while the *Paphiopedilum* and *Alocasia* 'Polly' assist in creating softer accents. They can be moved easily to open up additional seating in the room or to accommodate whatever the intention of the day might be. Yet another advantage of using multiple containers on a ledge: you can play freely with scale and proportion.

PLANTS SHOWN BELOW FROM LEFT: *ALOCASIA 'POLLY', PAPHIOPEDILUM, MONSTERA DELICIOSA*

PLANTS SHOWN FROM LEFT: *BEGONIA REX, ALOE, GYNURA*

MULTIPLE PLANTS,
ONE CONTAINER

A simple way to add complexity to an otherwise streamlined space is to use multiple types of plants in the same container. This requires a little bit of thought, but the impact is worth the extra effort. When arranging multiple plants in the same planter, you have to make sure they share similar light requirements. However, if you are drawn to a plant combination in which the light requirements are not perfectly aligned, just orientate the planter in such a way that the taller, light-loving plants are providing a little protection from the sun for their lower-growing, shade-loving roommates. Because the plants you choose for this type of planting are going to be living in close quarters with each other, their water and soil requirements need to be in the same range. Don't think of this as a limitation, but rather as a guide. More often than not plants that want full sun, dry soil, and ample drainage, for example, look great together. The same is true with low-light plants that come from humid tropical areas where rain is plentiful and the soil is always wet.

Picking the plants that are going to share the same container calls for a little bit of projection into the future. Most garden centers sell plants at varying stages of maturity. When you're choosing plants for the same container, consider the expected height and width of the plants when they're mature. Otherwise, a grouping that looks fantastic at the time of planting might, in time, become out of balance. If you are comfortable with your multiplant container being a temporary living arrangement, then you can be freer with your choices. If your goal is a long-lasting relationship, the way the plants will interact when they come into their own should be taken into account.

When we are choosing plants for a multiplant container, we usually start by picking the largest plant first. This plant will most likely hold the greatest visual weight in the planting, so let it be the plant that caught your eye—the one you can't do without. Then pick a companion. The companion should be a step down in size, but not a large step down. Both plants should be able to maintain their own identity, while at the same time work together to create a feel that is greater than the sum of their parts. Sometimes it is fine to stop at two plants, but usually three or more plants are needed to create pleasant cohesion. This is where the low-growing plants come into play. Small plants such *Pilea depressa*, *Soleirolia soleirolii*, or *Selaginella* can provide another level of color and texture. It is often these final touches that bring a planting to its full potential.

We've included a description on page 58 of how to create a multiplant container using three plants (*Alocasia* 'Polly', *Fittonia* 'Juanita', and *Pilea depressa*), but these same principles can be applied to groupings of four, five, or six plants and beyond. The key is to work from big to small. When you are actually placing the plants in their containers, work in this same order, from largest to smallest, because the larger plants will dictate the placement of the smaller ones. Before you reach that level of commitment, play around with different combinations. Use the floor of your garden center to stage your planting. Look at it up close and then step back to see if it has the same impact. Be picky. The perfect combination of plants for your container is out there, and with a little bit of effort you will find it.

PLANTS SHOWN OPPOSITE: *ALOCASIA* 'POLLY', *FITTONIA* 'JUANITA', *PILEA DEPRESSA*

MULTIPLE PLANTS,
ONE CONTAINER

MATERIALS LIST

Round, low-profile bowl at least 6″ deep and approximately 16″ in diameter

4-quart bag of gravel, such as small lava rock

12-quart bag of organic potting mix

Large-scale plant, preferably in a 6″ grower's pot (here we used *Alocasia* 'Polly')

Midsize plant, preferably in a 6″ grower's pot (here we used *Fittonia* 'Juanita')

Low-growing ground cover, preferably in a 4″ grower's pot (here we used *Pilea depressa*)

4-quart bag of live sheet moss

STEP 1 Begin by spreading a 1-inch layer of gravel at the bottom of the pot to serve as drainage.

STEP 2 Cover the rocks with a 2-inch layer of potting mix.

STEP 3 Remove the plants from their pots and carefully loosen the roots.

STEP 4 Place the plants in the bowl to gauge plant depth and arrangement. Remember to keep in mind how the plants grow with regard to scale and proportion. Don't place the tallest plant near the edge of the container or the shortest plant in the center. If viewed from one side, place the largest plant toward the back and the groundcover at the front of the container. Add more soil below the plants as needed to raise them to acceptable levels in the pot. The soil level in the new pot should be the same as the soil level in the grower's pots. Leave some space between the top of the planting and the top of your container, so that when you water, it won't flow out over the sides of the pot.

STEP 5 Fill in the remaining space around the plants with potting mix and tamp it down lightly to fill in any air pockets.

STEP 6 Top-dress the soil with sheet moss. This will allow the plants to fill in over time without crowding each other, but gives the impression of a full and lush planting.

For more on how to care for this project, see page 209.

Floor planters are one of the easiest ways to make a big impact in a room. They are like pieces of furniture and should be thought of as such when designing your space. Plants that live on the floor need to visually complement your existing decor, and they should be practical. Large floor plants can be the means to let a viewer's eye rest. They can also help define areas in an open floor plan. They can soften harsh angles, screen parts of the space that you want to hide, accentuate a room's best features, and add a textured surface to the existing palette.

III: ON THE FLOOR

PERSPECTIVE IS A KEY CONSIDERATION when planning the placement of floor plants. Pay attention to the layout of the room where you want to introduce some green. It's helpful to sketch the layout on a piece of paper, keeping in mind the most important viewpoints. Take note of where the furniture is placed and how it leads people through the room, physically and visually. Is there a spot that needs a focal point? Do you want to create a more welcoming point of entry? Concentrate on these areas and then strategize on what type of plants and containers could serve these purposes. Take note of how tall you want the plants to be in order for them to be viewed properly from various angles in the room. Some additional considerations are plant footprint and available light. Take measurements of the room so you know how much space you have to place a plant and still be able pass by it. Watch the light in the area (see table on page 184) and take into account any climate issues, such as the location of cooling or heating units, so you can pick out a plant that will visually and functionally fit the space. Now that you're familiar with the needs of the room, let's get started!

SOFTENING A ROOM

A lot of open space can sound like a dream, especially for apartment dwellers, but in reality a large open space can sometimes make a home feel bare and impersonal. For those who have a copious amount of open space in their home, incorporating big, tall, and lush plants into the decor is an excellent solution. There are many beautiful, sizable trees and palms that live quite well indoors. Whether you have floor-to-ceiling windows with bold direct sunlight, or a sweeping floor plan with just enough natural light to read by, large plants add another dimension to the space. They can change the way you approach and use an area by softening the room with their form and color.

We appreciate clean-lined design, but there are occasions that call for something to ease the angularity. What better than a potted plant? It can add visual comfort to right angles, edges, and corners. Sometimes you find yourself with unused pockets of space after arranging your furniture, especially if you've angled the furniture away from the walls. Fill those voids with houseplants to give them a sense of purpose.

If you are using your floor plants to fill a void or soften a minimalist environment, carefully consider your container selections. Used sensitively, they can complement their surroundings, uniting the plant and the layout. Take note of your selected plant's leaves. Each plant will have its own volume, determined by the amount and size of its leaves as well as its individual texture. Also pay attention to the overall height of the plant. Most large floor plants grow six to twelve inches per year. You do not want to place an eight-foot plant in a room with only nine-foot ceilings, as this could only be a temporary arrangement.

In the project to the left, a large *Polyscias balfouriana* is placed in the corner of a bedroom where it will receive bright, indirect light. The plant's variegated leaf pattern helps to keep the room light and airy while mirroring the look of the wallpaper. The white terrazzo stone container blends in with the room's concrete floor but contrasts with the green, making the plant the clear focus of the white-walled corner. Native to Southeast Asia, the aralia does well in a humid environment where it receives medium moisture or can dry out slightly in between waterings.

In the installation pictured on the next page, we planted a *Ficus lyrata* in a tall, sleek, solid-white container. *Ficus lyrata*, known as the fiddleleaf fig tree for its fiddle-shaped leaves, is one of the most popular indoor trees. Native to West Africa, this tropical tree thrives in full- to part-sun exposure and a short dry-out time between waterings. Their big, leathery, waxy green leaves have a remarkably lush aesthetic, complementing a range of interior styles. Here the white container blends into the space, keeping the area clean and open, while the large, dark green leaves of the *Ficus* balance out the visual weight of the loveseat. Although the leaves of the *Ficus* are solid and large, when placed in a white container, the plant almost floats above the seating area.

In large, open rooms with low to medium light, you can still house some sumptuous plants. The *Dracaena marginata* shown on page 67, otherwise known as the dragon tree, is favored for its thin, glossy green leaves with red edges. Incorporate this plant into your home or office as a statement piece—it will feel like a living sculpture. Some specimens have multiple stems emerging from the base like columns, and sometimes a grower will braid the plant's trunks as they mature. You can also find stumped forms, with a gnarled and mature trunk base. Don't worry too much about lighting with this plant, because it does well in low to medium light conditions and can be placed in a central room away from direct sun and windows. Watering is also a breeze as this plant can dry out two to four inches down between waterings.

PLANT SHOWN OPPOSITE: *POLYSCIAS BALFOURIANA*

With the right plant, a single large container can make a big difference in the feel of a space. The oversized leaves of *Schefflera actinophylla*, shown on page 68, give this plant a large physical character. The gorgeous glossy green leaves will draw your attention from across a room, as they fan out from the trunk, earning the plant its common name, umbrella tree. *Scheffleras* are terrific floor plants—they can tolerate a wide range of light conditions, but thrive with some morning or late-day direct sun. They also like a considerably long dry-out time between waterings (seven to fourteen days).

If a thicker visual buffer is needed to divide a space, a good option is *Chamaedorea seifrizii*, pictured on page 69, also known as the bamboo palm. These palms do very well in shady, low-light areas. The stalks display canelike markings similar to bamboo, but the foliage is denser. The bamboo palm is one of the best air-purifying plants available and is a good choice if you want an indoor palm that grows under ten feet in height.

PLANT SHOWN OPPOSITE: *FICUS LYRATA;* BELOW: *DRACAENA MARGINATA*

PLANT SHOWN: *SCHEFFLERA ACTINOPHYLLA 'AMATE'*

PLANT SHOWN: CHAMAEDOREA SEIFRIZII

NEED A WALL?

With an open floor plan, the options for laying out the space can seem limitless. However, this freedom can pose its own set of challenges. In an open floor plan, everything can be seen from multiple angles, and sometimes you need to create privacy or define an area. Do you need to screen off a bedroom, but constructing a wall is not an option? Or maybe you want to create a more formal entryway that affords your guests a moment of privacy before entering the room. Large floor plants can help; they can act as living walls without being overwhelming or confining.

When creating a living wall with floor plants, make it visually flawless and purposeful. We recommend using containers with similar styles to make a unified structure. One way to create a purposeful flow is to use long rectangular planters that can blend into a space seamlessly. Pay attention to the floor type (for example, hardwood or concrete) and color (dark or light), because the more you stay in tune with the room's palette, the more the containers will feel like a natural extension of the space.

In the project to the left, we planted *Phyllostachys*, or bamboo, in dark wood planters to match the rustic aesthetic of this hotel lobby. As the bamboo grows, it will continue to divide the two areas of the space, the front desk and the restaurant entryway. The height of the bamboo also helps to draw your eye upward and out of the long, linear lobby. Whenever you're working with a space that serves multiple functions, it's best to keep your configuration options open. The planters shown in this project also include wheels so that each planter can be moved around at will to accommodate more or less space for gathering in the lobby or restaurant.

Multiple container sizes can also be utilized to build a wall. The containers should be different heights, graduating down in size from highest to lowest, so that they step down toward the floor, softening the edge of an otherwise abrupt ending. For this style of wall, use planters that are the same color and made from the same material so they don't distract from the plants. However, the plant types do not need to be the same—feel free to use a variety of plant types in each container.

In the project below, *Monstera deliciosa* is used in the background planter to provide a solid, low-lying wall of greenery. *Microsorum diversifolium* (kangaroo fern) is used in the foreground rectangular container, providing a lush, light green hue that ties in with the stripes of the *Aglaonema* plant below. The flowering *Bougainvillea* tree adds height to disguise the post behind it as well as provides a pop of color for the neutral-toned office. A freestanding wall could have been constructed to segment the space, but by using blocks of plants, the room retains an element of softness and views are not fully obstructed.

PLANTS SHOWN OPPOSITE: *PHYLLOSTACHYS;* BELOW FROM LEFT: *MONSTERA DELICIOSA, MICROSORUM DIVERSIFOLIUM, AGLAONEMA, BOUGAINVILLEA*

BALANCING THE ZONE

Just as you can build a wall using floor planters, you can also use them to balance and frame a space. When you use floor planters to balance an area, take the relative height and proportions of the plants and the room into consideration. In order to create a sense of balance, it is important to keep a sense of unity. You want to create a visual buffer that directs the view, as opposed to obstructing the view.

In the room below, the dining room is separated from the living room by a low credenza. To help differentiate the two zones we installed two similarly colored planters. They frame the dining space and help ground the otherwise floating credenza. The taller plant (*Dracaena marginata*) is placed against the wall, and the shorter palm (*Howea forsteriana*) is placed by the credenza, to delineate the edge of the dining area, while not completely arresting the eye. Together, this arrangement divides the two areas while still allowing for ease of movement between them.

In the room to the left, the *Codiaeum variegatum* 'Banana' anchors the back corner while the *Dracaena marginata* flanks the front. The orange pots unify the space and provide a consistent color scheme throughout the room. With the lush foliage rising above the furniture, the plants cradle the living room and provide intimacy.

PLANTS SHOWN OPPOSITE FROM LEFT: *CODIAEUM VARIEGATUM, DRACAENA MARGINATA;*
BELOW FROM LEFT: *HOWEA FORSTERIANA, DRACAENA MARGINATA*

COMPOSING A PLANT FAMILY

Have you ever put a potted plant in its place, stood back, and thought, "Hmmm. This plant needs a friend?" Think about grouping a duo, trio, or even more when designing a floor plant arrangement. If you need height, but feel that a single potted plant might look like a ship lost at sea, grouping containers can be your SOS for a feeling of intentional design.

When planting containers that will be used in groups, consider the following: The planters should share a common feature, such as color or shape. Graduate the heights of the pots, from tallest to shortest. If necessary, you can accentuate the variation in height by using a plant stand. A grouping of containers in a range of sizes can have an organic effect, as if the pots themselves were living, multiplying beings.

Use plants in the same genus (all *Dracaena* for example), if you like, but vary the size of the plant itself when mixing container types and sizes. As shown opposite, we installed two different types and sizes of *Dracaena*, which mirror the form of the adjacent sculpture perfectly, while not distracting from it.

When you're using multiple containers, play their forms and colors off each other. In the installation pictured on p. 77, the taller *Dracaena* 'Limelight' is paired with a shorter *Anthurium*. The lime-colored leaves contrast with the gray and brown environment. At the same time, the plant's leaf shape and the color of the container echo the wall sculpture's color and form. Variation is most successful when differences can be seen within one or two elements, while similarities are maintained among others.

PLANTS SHOWN OPPOSITE FROM LEFT: *DRACAENA DEREMENSIS* 'LEMON LIME', *DRACAENA FRAGRANS* 'JANET CRAIG'

PLANT SHOWN AT CENTER: *PHILODENDRON SELLOUM*

PLANTS SHOWN FROM LEFT: *DRACAENA 'LIMELIGHT', ANTHURIUM*

DEFINE YOUR STYLE

Plants have their own personality. With its fuzzy white hair and its plodding growth, *Cephalocereus senilis* is truly an "old man cactus." *Adiantum capillus* or maidenhair fern is delicate, but vengeful if you forget her daily misting. Think about the statement you want your plants to make. How do you want to contextualize them? If your decor suggests a certain era, your containers can do the same. Whether your style is vintage, neoclassical, modern, industrial, or natural, there's a container that will fit perfectly in your space. Think of the shapes that were celebrated in the design era you favor. If you cannot find an original piece from that era, you can probably find a modern interpretation of its shape and form. Giving some thought to your existing decor before you buy any containers will reward you with containers that really work in your space and help prevent you from making an impulsive purchase that you'll regret later.

Here are a few of the design styles that we celebrate.

INDUSTRIAL Concrete floors, exposed ducts and pipes, and metal office furniture used as home furniture are a few of the hallmarks of an industrial aesthetic, which is often found in buildings that have been converted from a factory to a residence. Containers made from concrete, hypertufa, metal, or resin all conform to an industrial aesthetic and seamlessly fit in to any industrial space. Most of these materials are composed of a gray or brown color and provide a neutral base from which to design. This uncontrived aesthetic celebrates urban materials and textures, turning them into a vessel for plants. The result is a beautiful planter that has an effortless look, like the pot formed itself out of the construction debris. A plant will typically not evoke the atmosphere associated with heavy manufacturing, but a planter can. We look for planters whose material and construction can hang tough in a space. "Tough" does not necessarily imply blaring colors or a studded exterior, but something architectural that looks like you'd need steel-toed boots on if you wanted to kick it.

Even a soft silhouette can still have the personality that is needed to hold its own in an industrial space. The concrete fiber containers pictured on page 81 have an eloquent shape and understated color, but still make a strong and solid statement. In those, we paired a flowering *Begonia* with other large-leafed plants. Their broad-leaf shapes contrast with the hard material of the planters and the space itself. Together the plant and container are the kind of unexpected combination that thrives in a raw-looking space.

The planters pictured opposite also work well in an industrial space. Made from aluminum, their geometric shapes can easily be placed center stage so that their forms can be studied and admired from multiple angles. Their tough exterior will wow onlookers—they're objects of art themselves.

PLANTS SHOWN OPPOSITE FROM LEFT: *FICUS ELASTICA, ASPARAGUS SPRENGERI, EPIPREMNUM* 'NEON'

PLANT SHOWN: *CYCAS REVOLUTA*

PLANTS SHOWN FROM LEFT:
BEGONIA REX, MEDINILLA MAGNIFICA

MIDCENTURY MODERN Its clean simplicity blends well with many other styles. Architects associated with this design movement emphasized bringing the outdoors in, which resulted in a corresponding wealth of plant containers. Post-and-beam construction, a key motif of the style, is reflected in these containers; often pots from that era are composed of two separate pieces—the legs (or stand) and the vessel—instead of one solid piece. We like to use updated, spun aluminum versions of these classics, tipping our plant hat to this characteristic style. These containers suit almost any plant, though we've found that *Philodendron* 'Moonlight' and *Howea forsteriana* (kentia palm) have a midcentury look, seeming as if they could have come straight out of an episode of *Mad Men*. When you have a statement piece of furniture, such as the chair above, it is important that the plants provide their own statement. Where once the chair seemed to float alone in the corner, it is now surrounded by complementary pieces of green that help set the tone for the seating area.

It can be a challenge to bring in floor plants if there are too many elements or styles in a living space. If that's the case, utilize containers that will harken back to a certain era, but also act as a connection to the various elements in the room. The arching fronds of *Cycas revoluta*, or sago palm, in the room on page 80 help connect the rectangular elements of the shelf and chair. At the same time, it does not impede the art or shelving display visually.

NATURALIST When you crave a connection to the outdoors, do more than just bring a plant inside—choose a container that celebrates the natural world. Naturalist containers can be literal or figurative. You can use the shape of an object found in nature such as an apple or pineapple as a model for a vessel, or you can take an actual object from nature like a tree trunk and turn it into a planter. Whichever direction you choose, explore the organic textures and shapes that mimic what you would find outside. Naturalist vessels are usually neutral in color and have an unfinished, textural quality.

In the project below, a mixture of real and manufactured bark containers are used to house a collection of small houseplants. The plant selections for naturalist containers generally work best if the plants are woodland ferns, mosses, or other dark green foliage, as brightly colored tropical plants can appear kitschy or artificial. Don't worry if you don't have access to actual tree stumps to turn into containers— using a fiberglass tree form can still allow you to appreciate the imperfections in nature. Rough textures, natural colors, and organic shapes are what you're looking for and what makes it beautiful.

PLANTS SHOWN OPPOSITE FROM LEFT: *PHILODENDRON 'MOONLIGHT', HOWEA FORSTERIANA, AGLAONEMA, SPATHIPHYLLUM*; BELOW FROM LEFT: *PHILODENDRON SELLOUM, ADIANTUM, PAPHIOPEDILUM, ALOCASIA 'POLLY'*

NEOCLASSICAL Chances are you do not live in a Louis XIV–style home, but you admire the grandeur and opulence of the style. A return to the classics is never a bad idea, so why not consider it with your plant container? Introducing a classic design allows you to play with the aesthetics of the room, so instead of donning a powdered wig, give your space a taste of the Age of Enlightenment with a well-placed classical floor urn. You can embrace the neoclassical look by keeping things balanced and orderly, or you can play with the design by adding in other styles such as post-modernism or minimalism.

Neoclassical containers can make a highly stylized statement in a room, and when potted with the right plant they can be a real showpiece. Though traditionally shaped, these urns and containers can work in many different settings. One way to update a neoclassical urn for a contemporary setting is to celebrate the form but play with the color or texture (or both) of the pot. Try painting it a solid color to make its shape stand out even further. In the project opposite, the urn-shaped vessels have been treated with a bright yellow rubber paint. The yellow color makes the deep green plants pop. The *Mandevilla* vine in the taller pot provides a lush, just-picked look with its outstretched tendrils. The shorter *Aglaonema* with its upright, arching shape also highlights the urn's stately nature. This bold treatment of something traditional mixed with something natural brings an opulent feel to a room without committing to recreating Versailles.

PLANTS SHOWN OPPOSITE FROM LEFT: *AGLAONEMA, MANDEVILLA*

The ceiling is an area that's often overlooked for displaying plants in a home or office. Just like a wall or ledge, it is yet another way to find space if your tabletop and floor area is limited. It is also a good solution if your pets think your plants are their personal buffet. Suspending plants from the ceiling is a great way to add green to your enviornment and can have a huge impact, while still providing the freedom to be creative. Think of them as living curtains that can be strategically placed to frame a space. They can be a statement piece, a little oasis, or an object of desire—it is your choice.

IV: IN THE AIR

THE MOST IMPORTANT CONSIDERATION HERE is making sure that your ceiling can support hanging plants. If you rent, get permission from your landlord before you begin drilling. It is also important to find out if there are electrical lines or air ducts that you should avoid. When securing planters to the ceiling, find a joist or stud to secure the hook that you'll be using to hang your plants. If you cannot find one, hang a very light container or use anchors.

Also, consider how high to hang the plants before you begin drilling into the ceiling. You do not want to create an obstacle course through your home for your tall friends! Measure the diameter of both the plant and container to allow enough space on either side after it is hung. This planning will be well worth your time as it prevents having to make adjustments later.

Another practical and important consideration is the ease with which you can reach the plants to care for them. If you hang them at a level that requires a ladder to access them, select plants that can handle drying out between waterings—then you won't have to use the ladder as frequently.

Drainage is a consideration for hanging plants too. If the container has a drain hole but no built-in saucer, you'll need to remove the container and take it to a sink or bathtub, or outside, in order to water it. If the container has a drain hole with a built-in saucer, then just be careful that the saucer does not overflow when you're watering. If the container doesn't have any built-in drainage, create drainage (see page 187).

Now, after considering your container, and the logistics of hanging something from the ceiling, you can think about your plant options. Some plants are better suited to hanging than others. We recommend using trailing vines that will cascade down to the floor, or climb their way up to the ceiling. Remember to consider how the plant will grow over time. Even though you know that a certain plant will trail, take a look at mature examples so you can see what it will look like when it's full-grown.

Good options for hanging plants include *Aeschynanthus, Bougainvillea, Chlorophytum, Cissus, Dischidia, Epipremnum, Ficus pumila, Gynura, Hedera helix, Hoya, Passiflora, Peperomia, Philodendron, Rhipsalis, Setcreasea pallida, Stephanotis,* and *Tradescantia* among others.

PLANT SHOWN OPPOSITE: *AESCHYNANTHUS LOBBIANUS* 'RASTA'

MODERN MACRAMÉ

The plant and container are not the only aesthetic considerations. The hanging mechanism itself, such as rope or cord material, contributes to the finished style of the hanging plant. For lightweight vessels that are less than two pounds, use fishing line for a floating effect. Wire cable, which you can purchase by the foot at a hardware store, gives a solid, sleek look to the hanging arrangement. Or, consider using steel chain for an industrial feel. For a more natural approach, we like using leather, yarn, cotton twine, and other materials that can be highly manipulated and tactile. The options are boundless, and each can impact the demeanor of your hanging garden. And who says that it has to be only one string hanging down to support your plants? What if there were multiple cords acting in unison? Yes, we are talking about macramé (see page 92 for project).

Whether you are living in a small apartment in Brooklyn, a farmhouse in Oklahoma, or a beach house in California, hanging planters with macramé can save on space and add texture to a room or patio. A modern take on macramé deconstructs the shaggy, yellow owls of decades past to one simple element: the knot. There is something so pure and simple about this nostalgic, utilitarian, yet stylish craft. Before its comeback in the 1970s, macramé had nearly become extinct. Currently, macramé is making yet another comeback and we love all of the new, modern takes on this classic craft.

Pictured opposite and below is a macramé construction using cotton cord with colored thread wrapped around it to create patches of color that break up the vertical lines of the space. The small pop of color against the natural cotton cord is soft enough to work with any style of decor, from bohemian to modern. The glass vessels are great for showcasing the lines of the macramé. *Stephanotis floribunda*, with its beautiful waxy, deep green leaves, is the perfect complement to the twist and curves of the wild trailing *Hoya* plant. The macramé envelops each planting and highlights the natural ease of the plants beautifully.

PLANTS SHOWN: *HOYA 'HINDU ROPE' SURROUNDED BY STEPHANOTIS FLORIBUNDA*

MACRAMÉ HOLDER

MATERIALS LIST

Three 100" lengths of
³⁄₁₆"-thick cotton cord

1" to 1¼" brass ring
or key chain ring

Hook or nail
affixed to a wall
(to hold macramé
while you work)

Scissors

Colored string

8" glass bowl

Rocks for drainage
(we recommend lava rock)

Potting soil

Plants suitable for
an 8" container
(such as *Stephanotis*
and *Hoya* plants)

Decorative moss
(optional)

STEP 1 Slide all three cords through the metal ring until the ring is at their midpoint. If you hold the ring up, you'll have six cords to work with, each 50 inches in length.

STEP 2 Use all six lengths to tie a knot tightly against the ring. Make the knot as tight as possible by pulling on each cord individually.

STEP 3 Hang the ring on a hook or nail affixed on a wall. This will allow you to use both of your hands while you work.

STEP 4 Divide the cords into three groups of two. Tie a simple knot in each pair 18 inches below the ring. You will have three knots that line up horizontally. Make sure each knot is tight.

STEP 5 Take one string from two adjacent knotted pairs, and tie them together in a knot about 5 inches down from the previous knot.

STEP 6 Repeat step 5 until all of the bundles are tied together. This creates a zigzag pattern among the cords.

STEP 7 About 5 or 6 inches below the second set of knots, tie all six lengths together to make one large final knot. Pull each cord individually to ensure that the knot is as tight as possible.

STEP 8 Use scissors to trim the cords to your desired length.

STEP 9 Wrap the colored string around individual cords to create 4-inch blocks of color (or any length that you like). Tie it off in a knot and cut any excess string. Now that you've completed your macramé hanger, you can begin planting the container.

STEP 10 Place about 1 inch of lightweight rocks into the bottom of the glass bowl. Fill the bowl with 3 inches of potting soil.

STEP 11 Remove the plant from its container and massage the roots to loosen the soil. Place the plant into the glass bowl and fill in the sides with potting soil, then pat down the soil firmly. Place decorative moss on top of the soil (optional).

STEP 12 Place the bowl directly above the lowest knot and pull up the sides of the cords to create a web for it to rest on. Pull any long plant stems through the macramé to ensure the plant is sitting evenly on all sides.

For more on how to care for this project, see page 209.

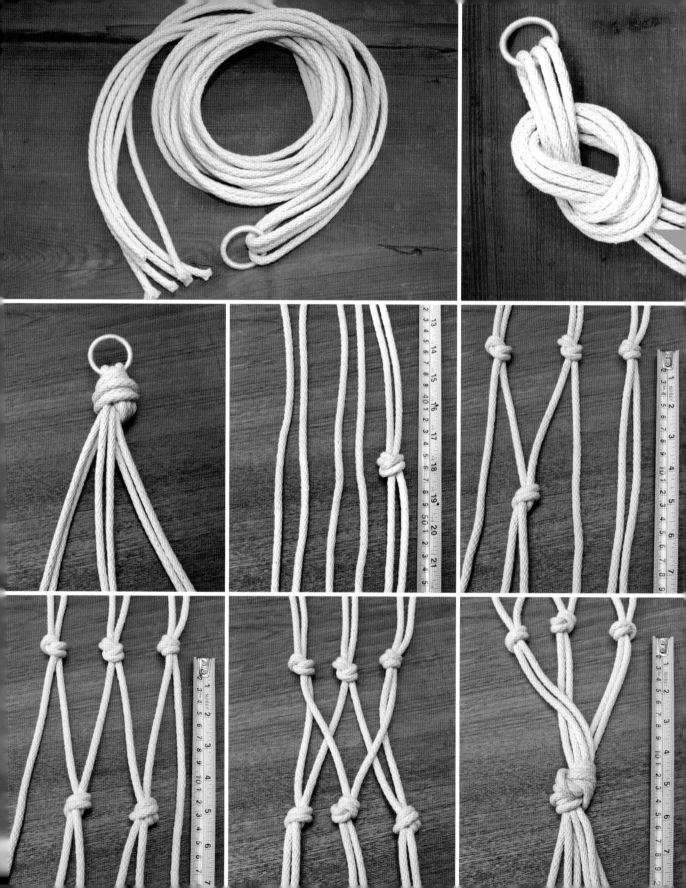

KOKEDAMA

Kokedama is a free-form planting method that derives from bonsai, which is the practice of training and manipulating small trees and shrubs to evoke the majesty of their ancient counterparts found in nature. Kokedama has intrigued the garden and craft world with its versatility and inherent charm. It involves wrapping a plant's roots with soil and moss to create something that looks like a living sculpture. Kokedamas are designed to dangle; by suspending them in the air with colorful twine, you can create a hanging garden for inside your home or even outdoors in the warmer seasons (see project page 96). They can also sit on a shallow dish for display.

Kokedamas are wrapped in an exterior layer of moss. Select plants that will work well in an environment that provides bright but indirect natural light. Direct sun will cause kokedamas to dry out and fade quickly. Ideal options are *Anthurium*, *Epipremnum pinnatum*, ferns, *Ficus pumila*, *Fittonia*, most orchids, *Philodendron*, *Pilea*, *Peperomia*, and *Selaginella*, among others. As an alternative for sunnier locations, consider using preserved moss instead of living and choose your plants accordingly.

PLANTS SHOWN OPPOSITE FROM LEFT: *RHIPSALIS, HEDERA, PEPEROMIA, PLATYCERIUM, PHILODENDRON*

KOKEDAMA

MATERIALS LIST

1 small houseplant
in 4″ pot

Pruners

An 8:3 ratio of peat
moss and bonsai soil
(for a 4″ plant use
2 cups peat moss,
¾ cup bonsai soil)

Plastic grocery bag
or small bucket

A small container
of water

Gloves (optional)

Sphagnum moss for
wrapping the soil

Strong string or twine

Sheet moss (dried or
live, depending on
your project)

STEP 1 Gently remove the plant from the pot that it came in. Remove the soil from the roots until most of the soil is fully separated from the root system. Plants with finer root systems may need to be rinsed in the sink to help remove the soil. Prune the roots and leaves to the size you want.

STEP 2 Mix together the peat moss and bonsai soil in a plastic grocery bag or bucket. (Wear gloves if you like.) Add small splashes of water as you mix. Keep mixing until the mixture can be formed into a firm ball of soil with your hands.

STEP 3 Form a ball of soil that is big enough to encase the root system of the plant. Set it aside.

STEP 4 Wrap a layer of dried sphagnum moss entirely around the plant's root system. The plant's roots will grow into this layer.

STEP 5 Using string or twine, secure the layer of sphagnum moss to the plant by wrapping the string around the moss several times and tying it off.

STEP 6 With your fingertip, create a hole in the ball of soil that is big enough to insert the sphagnum-wrapped root system into. Carefully put the wrapped root system in the hole and re-form the ball until it is nice and solid.

STEP 7 Using the sheet moss, cover every part of the soil sphere, and wrap it securely several times with twine or string. Be sure to tie it off when you are done. Leave on some extra length if you would like to use this same string or twine to hang your finished kokedama.

STEP 8 The same string or twine may be used to display your plant. Attaching a thin chain or decorative cord to the wrapping can serve as a mechanism to hang the kokedama.

STEP 9 Before hanging your kokedama, make sure to soak it in a bowl of water. The living moss and plant will benefit from the moisture.

For more on how to care for this project, see page 209.

PLANT SHOWN: *NEPHROLEPSIS CORDIFOLIA 'DUFFII'*

PLANT SHOWN: *PHALAENOPSIS*

MARIMO

Marimo, or *Aegagropila linnaei*, are spheres of pure green algae that form naturally in cool lakes in the Northern Hemisphere, specifically in Iceland, Scotland, Japan, and Estonia. Velvety in appearance, these little mysteries can be wonderful houseplants and are perfect to use in clear hanging vessels.

They will move up and down in the vessel as they photosynthesize, but it is a very slow process so you might not even notice any movement. But you don't need to see them moving in order to enjoy them. If the hanging container you are using is at eye level or lower, use something to visually ground them. Material such as decorative rock is the perfect complement to a *marimo*, adding weight to the container while being easy to keep clean. (Using more granular material, like sand, will cause the water to become dirty.) Whatever material you select, make sure to thoroughly clean it. We recommend staying away from any decorative green material as this will blend in with the *marimo* instead of contrasting with them. If the vessel is being hung above eye level, forgo using any additional material in it, as you do not want to block the *marimo* from being viewed.

The trick to caring for *marimo* is to keep them clean and cool. They are used to being on the bottom of cool lakes rolling around on the lake bed to keep their shape. When they're in a contained environment, they need to be kept out of the direct sun—not only will it burn the *marimo*, but it will also heat up the water, which in turn will make the water dirty. Change the water at least once a week with slightly cooler water. Give the balls a slight squeeze and let them roll around when doing so to help them keep their natural form. We also like to add a drop of aquatic water cleaner to keep the water clear and a drop of aquatic fertilizer once a month from spring to fall to help feed them.

We get a lot of questions at Sprout Home about *marimo*, and once people realize that they are indeed not fake, they almost always want to know if they can put them in their fish tank. We don't recommend putting *marimo* in a fish tank. Most fish are grass eaters and will treat a moss ball like a self-serve buffet. You can pair the moss balls with fish that don't eat grass, such as betta fish, but you'll have to change the water frequently to keep it clean and fresh.

PLANT SHOWN OPPOSITE: *AEGAGROPILA LINNAEI*

CHANDELIER

One mature hanging plant can certainly have a singularly large impact on a space, but so can a collection of smaller plants hung together to make an overhead garden. When you're figuring out a design for your hanging garden, play with a multitude of heights. If you want to use multiple plants in a hanging garden, we recommend using a thin cord to hang the plants because it will blend into the space and not distract from the plants. For smaller containers, fishing wire or other clear wire will work.

This type of installation transforms a group of small hanging containers into a chandelier-shaped garden. It can work in a space like a piece of furniture would, spotlighting a certain area and drawing attention to it. Its complexity can add intrigue and depth to an otherwise empty void, and it works best in a surrounding that is calling for visual texture. The most important aspect to installing multiple hanging containers is figuring out how to hang them so that they harmonize visually. You can always hang the vessels spaced evenly apart, but it's probably more desirable to have a little bit of randomness, especially when you're using a variety of plant types. Even if you use an arrangement that looks somewhat staggered, you'll still want the placement to appear purposeful. Don't hang them so randomly that the grouping looks like a mistake—it will break the harmony. Take note of the various viewing angles of the hanging garden, and make sure that no containers are obstructed from view from any perspective. Ask a friend to help you—they can hold the cords in place as you move around the garden to make sure it is hanging at the right height and depth from all sides. Start with the larger hanging vessels and work your way to the smaller ones. It might even be useful to use paper cutouts suspended with string to help you envision what the final product will be. They can be moved around until they are just right, and when your plants are ready to hang you can replace the cutouts one by one with the real thing.

Try to coordinate your hanging planters with another color already found in the room. The hanging gold vessels in the project opposite coincide with the fluorescent gold light suspended from the ceiling and the gold stripe in the painting. Other color options for this space include white, blue, or pink, as these would also tie in with the painting. If your space does not already have a fixture from which to hang plants, you can mount the hanging plants directly into the ceiling using ceiling hooks.

The pictured arrangement is in part sun, and uses containers with a shallow depth. *Begonia*, *Pilea*, and ferns are a great choice for shallow containers. Their sculptural nature adds more form and architecture to the sleek and simple pots. When planting in multiples, it's best to use at least two or three of the same type of plant so that the overall grouping looks cohesive. It will also make the singular types of plants used stand out more. If the purpose of a chandelier is to give light to a room, the purpose of a chandelier garden is to provide radiant greenery.

PLANTS SHOWN OPPOSITE: FERN, *PILEA DEPRESSA, SAXIFRAGA*

THROUGH THE LOOKING GLASS SIDEWAYS

Do you have a window that has equal importance whether you are viewing it from the inside or outside? Maybe you want to add some plant life to create a welcoming vibe to people walking by outside, without the plants being in your way on the inside. The perfect solution is to frame the window space with hanging containers. This is a great opportunity to create a window display without weighing down the frame of the scene inside, and it will still allow you ample room inside to enjoy yourself.

As with the other hanging constructions we've discussed, consider all the angles from which the planters will be viewed. Plants tend to grow in the direction of the light, so you'll need to rotate the plants regularly so that you have equally long tendrils on all sides. And who says that hanging planters always have to have plants coming through the top of the pot? Look beyond the traditional planter to other objects that can serve as vessels. Why not a collection of birdhouses? Feel free to use whatever has the perfect proportions for your project and the character you are looking for. Let the inspiration of the room speak to you when you're looking for containers. If you select a container that has an opening on the side, be sure that it has enough depth for the soil and plant roots. The soil line can only come up so far in a container with a hole in its side because otherwise you'll have soil pouring out of the hole. We recommend a depth of at least two inches for succulents and at least three inches for low-growing ground covers.

In the design opposite, the hexagonal birdhouse has been repurposed into a hanging planter. Since the birdhouse has a hole on only one side (facing in to the room), it's best to use plants that splay out in multiple directions so that viewers can see a little bit of greenery no matter what angle they view it from. Trailing plants will provide a lusher, tropical feel. Succulents, with their angular geometric shapes, would be a good way to play off of the hexagonal shape of the birdhouse.

In addition to considering vessels with interesting shapes, think about interesting colors. Would your window benefit from having a pop of color, or would a neutral tone work better? Hanging containers can help bring focus to a window or area that one might pass by without ever noticing it.

Plants that can handle a shallow planting depth and a low-medium light scenario are *Epipremnum pinnatum*, *Ficus pumila*, *Hedera helix*, *Muehlenbeckia*, *Pilea glauca*, and *Setcreasea pallida* 'Purple Heart'. For full-sun areas, consider using *Agave*, *Aloe*, *Crassula*, *Echeveria*, *Sedum*, *Sempervivum*, and *Senecio*.

When watering hanging plants, we recommend using a watering can that has a long narrow neck. You should also be cautious and pour slowly when you're watering a container with a side planting hole, because water may run off and spill out, instead of being absorbed by the soil. You can also use a spritzer on a very focused setting (instead of a general mist) in order to saturate the soil and reach the roots of the plant.

PLANTS SHOWN BELOW FROM LEFT: *SEDUM, FICUS PUMILA, STEPHANOTIS FLORIBUNDA*

We spend much of our time at tables. Whether you are sitting down to dinner with guests, typing away at a computer, or just reaching for your TV remote, you will benefit from giving some thought to this often-neglected space. Because there is minimal installation required for a tabletop, and because tabletops are highly visible, the style of the containers is the key creative variable. When the right container is matched with the right plant, the pairing becomes living art. Because a container can be such a focal point for table plants, it deserves special consideration.

V: ON THE TABLE

WE'D LIKE TO TAKE A MOMENT to address a classic dilemma: "Which comes first—the container or the plant?" When making decisions about which botanical creations to introduce into your home, there are a lot of directions to go, but many of us get stuck at this first juncture. Sometimes your top priority is just to get some green into your home. In this case, let your heart guide you to a plant that you feel an affinity toward, then select a suitable container to house that plant. If you have particular environmental conditions in your space, such as low light, let them lead you to a plant first, container second. (See page 183 for more information on how to determine your light).

Starting with a container is usually the best option if you are approaching plants from a design perspective. When you are looking for that key component to bring the aesthetic of a room together, it is often best to begin with the container. From there, select a plant of complementary size and shape. The problem comes when you are not sure which to start with. Our advice? Avoid second-guessing and honor whichever situation is your priority: design or the right plant for the conditions in your home. That being said, there are moments when a container catches your eye and trumps everything else.

Whether you are starting with a container or a plant, there are several practical issues you should take into consideration. First, what size container are you looking for? Most tabletop containers are relatively small, holding four- to six-inch diameter pots. Sometimes you may want to create height and use the plant as a focal point in a room, but keep in mind your size constraints. As a plant's height increases, so does the size of its base. To accommodate a large plant with an existing eight- to ten-inch diameter, you will need to get an even larger container—one that is a couple of inches larger in diameter than its current pot. For tall plants, make sure your container has a stable base or is made from a material that is heavy enough to support the plant.

The second thing to keep in mind is drainage. Sure that herb looks good planted in a teacup, but where will all the water go? Does your pot have a drain hole and saucer? If not, you will need to create faux drainage with small rocks and select plants that require minimal watering. Another option is to leave your plant in its plastic grower's pot and set it in a cachepot. This arrangement does not allow for much growth, but if you have a young plant, you may be able to leave it in its current pot for a while.

PLANTS SHOWN OPPOSITE FROM LEFT: *APHELANDRA SQUARROSA*, *EUCHARIS X GRANDIFLORA*

Another practical consideration to make is the weight of your container. If your table (or your arms!) are not industrial strength, select lightweight containers such as rice pots, pots made from resin, or pots made from plastic. If weight is not an issue, there are many great materials to work with including concrete, ceramic, wood, and metal.

Now we are ready to talk about the look and feel of the container. Think about color and texture. Where will the container be placed? Are you going to see it, or will it be covered with a trailing plant? Do you want something smooth and glossy, or would a natural texture work better for your space? What feelings do you want to evoke? These are all issues to consider when creating a tabletop planting.

If you do decide to start with the plant selection before a container, make sure you consider where the plant will be placed. For dining tables, you'll want to keep plantings low so they don't interfere with the view across the table. For tables against a wall, you can select plants that have more height to them. Long, rectangular tables generally look better with linear plants down the center. You can stagger these at different heights to provide added interest, or keep them all at one height to create a more uniform look. For round tables, group three or five various-size plants together (odd numbers look best). This will fill out the unused space in the center of the table and provide viewing points from multiple angles. The types of plants available for tabletop usage are as numerous as the container options. Your best method of selecting the right plant is to choose one based on your light. For more information on determining what type of light you have, see page 183. Once the plant is selected, it's time to find the perfect pot!

PLANTS SHOWN OPPOSITE FROM LEFT: *ALOCASIA 'POLLY', PAPHIOPEDILUM, SAXIFRAGA*

CONTAINER STYLES

After being in the plant business for more than a decade, there are days when we think we might have seen every indoor plant imaginable. Thankfully, we are proven wrong time and time again. However, when it comes to containers, the "seen it all" mentality subsides. The number of plants that are appropriate for an indoor setting might be finite, but the different types of containers available seems to be endless. That said, there are certain styles we keep coming back to. What follows is a list of our favorites, but it is by no means exhaustive. Use it as a guide, but don't stop here.

CLEAN AND SIMPLE If you favor a spare, streamlined decor, selecting modern container groupings can play a pivotal role in keeping things simple. With the extraneous details pared away, let the plants speak for themselves in a monochromatic or understated container.

Pay attention to the colors of the room you're bringing plants into. If you want to simplify your room's palette, select containers with the same hue as the space. By doing so, you will obtain a symbiotic relationship between the space and the container, allowing the existing color scheme to play the predominant role.

Are there textures in your space that share a similar pattern? You can pick up and reiterate these patterns and textures with your pot selection as well to create a more harmonious plant grouping. Or perhaps, as you look around your space, you find that there is a lot going on visually and you'd like to simplify it. You know you want to introduce some greenery, but you don't want any additional "noise." In this situation, we recommend that you simplify your container options. Think about clean lines that don't fight with the existing surroundings but provide cohesion. Refrain from introducing another color scheme with your pots. Instead, find a commonality to work within that is already present in the room's decor. If your room has dominant blue tones, stick with a monochromatic blue color palette for all of your containers.

PLANTS SHOWN OPPOSITE: *AGLAONEMA*; PLANT SHOWN BELOW: *ECHEVERIA*

FOUND OBJECT PLANTER Do you find yourself collecting random household objects unsure of how to utilize them in your everyday life? Many people have collections of toys, tin cans, teapots, and birdcages that they're just waiting to do something with. A found object like this can be easily transformed. Who says you have to use it for its original purpose? You are the one who found it, right? Go ahead and turn it into a planter. It can be as simple as creating a hole to accommodate the plant's roots.

To test if your found object is watertight, fill it with water and look for leaks. If it does leak, you can use silicone (available at hardware stores) to caulk the areas where water is escaping. After giving the silicone twenty-four hours to cure, fill the bottom of the object with a layer of rocks for drainage and transplant a plant into it. In some cases, your found object will be able to withstand a hole being drilled into it. Make sure you have the appropriate drill bit for the material; then you'll have the ease of having a drain in your new, repurposed planter. (But you'll need to water it in a sink or tub, or set it on something that will act as a saucer. Perhaps another found object that can serve as a saucer?) After doing the initial preparation, have fun giving new life to something that already brings you pleasure.

GEO ANGULAR Geometric designs have a strong three-dimensional language that challenges our assumptions of form and functionality. Traditional ceramic techniques of hand molding and wheel throwing usually result in circular-shaped pots, which are, of course, very popular. With new pot-making techniques such as granulate pressing, injection molding, pressure casting, and slip casting, more designers are experimenting with complex geometric shapes, as seen on page 116. Now, the possibilities seem endless: prisms, tetrahedrons, dodecahedron, and parallelepipeds, to name a few! Planters made in these bold shapes become the focal point in any room. A great geometric planter does not require any colorful glaze or additional decorative elements—its shape alone provides the interest. We love pairing plants with these planters because of the tension between a natural element and a manmade one. It can result in an electric combination, and a big statement for your small (or large) table.

PLANTS SHOWN OPPOSITE, CLOCKWISE FROM TOP RIGHT: *HEMIONITIS ARIFOLIA; SEDUM; SAXIFRAGA; EUPHORBIA, CACTI; KALANCHOE THRYSIFLORA, CRASSULA, ECHEVERIA, AGAVE*

PLANTS SHOWN FROM LEFT: *ASPLENIUM, ZAMIOCULCAS ZAMIIFOLIA*

PLANT SHOWN:
TRADESCANTIA MULTIFLORA

INDUSTRIAL SOLID Not all containers are made from ceramic or plastic. When you're making a container selection, consider the fact that materials like concrete and metal can also be turned into pots. Concrete and metal containers can impart a sense of visual weightiness but are usually not physically as heavy as they look. They have an association with all that is solid and dependable, and they're tactile. Think of Greek or Roman statuary, or public sculptures by Picasso; these pieces are built to last. These materials can work in almost any style of decor. Their ruggedness allows for an uncomplicated, effortless look, as if you just mixed up a batch of concrete in your living room or welded that sheet metal together on your lunch break. Who doesn't do that on their lunch break?

The percentage of actual concrete mix used in concrete containers varies, so keep their weight in mind when you're looking at them. One way to gauge this is to simply lift up the container. Consider how much that container will weigh when it is filled with moist soil and a plant, and make sure your tabletop will be able to physically support your potted plant. There are lighter-weight concrete blends available on the market. If you are using or making concrete containers, be aware that unless they're treated, they will absorb moisture and condensation.

VINTAGE When you're creating a look for your home or office, select something that is unique to your personality. We've found that vintage containers always have something special—an individual character that is hard to reproduce. Each vintage vessel seems to have a story, and it is a lot of fun pairing plants with vintage containers. We love finding gems at thrift shops, secondhand stores, and flea markets. You never know what you will find! And when you do find "the one," you will know, because it speaks to you—it will make you smile and ponder the possibilities. When we have these moments at a local garage sale, the first and only question we ask each other is "Can it accomodate a plant?" and if it can, game on!

PLANTS SHOWN OPPOSITE: *ALBUGA LONGIFOLIA*; BELOW: *GYNURA*

PLANTS SHOWN: *HEDERA HELIX, FERNS, CRASSULA, CACTI*

While some containers are chosen because they blend in, vintage containers usually scream for attention, and we believe they should receive the recognition they deserve. Accommodating a pot's shape, style, and unique features is always key when selecting plants, but in the case of vintage containers, they can be even more important. Select companion plants that complement, but don't hide, a vintage container—give it the same top billing as the plant, such as the combination on page 117.

Sometimes the shape, color, and texture of a tabletop container are all you need to create a vintage aesthetic (without really being vintage). Opposite is a blend of vintage and contemporary containers with potted plants that work together to create a unified, pale dusk color story. The matte groove on the blue pot (which is not vintage) adds a textural element, while the rounded bowl, although a different shape than its taller counterpart, is still consistent with the color theme. All of these containers are of the same hue and can be rearranged without offsetting the natural balance.

FROM LEFT: *SEDUM, CRASSULA, AEONIUM 'SCHWARZKOPF', DRIMIOPSIS MACULATA*

BRANCH IT OUT

Cut flowers are beautiful yet short-lived additions to a decorative tablescape. As an alternative to floral arrangements, consider using wood-mounted air plants or other bromeliads to liven up the table at your next dinner party. *Tillandsia* come in nearly as wide an array of shapes and colors as cut flowers, and can be perched on beautiful branches or mounted on pieces of driftwood for a lasting, living addition to your dining room or kitchen table. *Tillandsia* is a varied group of plants, native to the humid areas of the southern United States and tropical Central and South America. Many varieties will produce vibrant blooms and grow new offshoots for a constantly changing display.

A driftwood centerpiece mounted with epiphytes (plants that grow on other plants) will not only be beautiful, but will mimic *Tillandsia*'s natural habitat. You can even mount small *Phalaenopsis* orchids to the centerpiece for a more colorful and floral feel. Most components can be secured to a piece of driftwood using fishing line or thin floral wire. Clumps of moss on top of the branch serve as anchor points for the plants and provide a receptacle for moisture. Lightly moistened, long-fibered sphagnum moss (sometimes sold as orchid moss), Spanish moss, or sheet moss can be used. For a fuller look, consider draping Spanish moss (also in the *Tillandsia* genus) over the wood. Decorative features, such as dried flowers or cut succulents, should be added last to give the arrangement a more gardenlike appearance.

Once you have everything arranged on the driftwood, make sure your centerpiece is in a place that receives bright, indirect light. *Tillandsia* should also receive a soaking according to the climate of your home. With a little creativity and a few simple elements, your centerpiece can be a beautiful and natural addition to your home. But watch out, this type of display is contagious. Pretty soon everything you own will be covered in little bits of moss and air plants, which, in our opinion, is not a bad thing.

PLANTS SHOWN OPPOSITE: MIXED *TILLANDSIA*; BELOW: *DRIMIOPSIS MACULATA*, DRIED *ECHINOPS*

We think everyone should grow at least one fresh ingredient to cook with. Growing edible plants in your home or workspace brings plant care to an entirely new level. Now you're growing plants that benefit your health as well as your environment. In this chapter, we'll highlight plants that are terrific both aesthetically and aromatically and are well suited for indoor growing. We'll also discuss medicinal plants that are helpful to have on hand for bug bites and burns, and those that make a delicious cup of tea. We'll show examples of containers that are functional and, when paired with the right plants, can create stunning edible gardens.

VI: IN THE KITCHEN

INDOOR EDIBLE GARDENS often fail because of inadequate light, drainage, or container space. We've all been tempted to grow herbs in tiny containers without drainage (think cute teacup gardens), but edible plants need more room to grow. Below are some basic guidelines to follow when you're growing herbs or veggies indoors. There's more information in Chapter VIII: The Roots.

LIGHT First, edibles grown indoors need plenty of sun—it's a losing battle to try to grow edibles without adequate sunlight. A south- or west-facing exposure with direct sun hitting the plants for a minimum of five hours per day is best. If you do not have enough light, you can supplement with grow lights. If your space only has part-sun exposure, and there's no way around it, try growing arugula, cilantro, lemon balm, mint, parsley, Swiss chard, sorrel, or tarragon; these plants do not require a lot of direct sun.

WATER In addition to ample sunlight, most edibles need a lot of water and all require excellent drainage, so make sure that any container you choose has adequate drain holes. Put some rocks in the bottom of the container if you think the drain holes are too small or in danger of becoming clogged. To avoid spilling water onto the floor, place a big saucer under the container so that any excess water has somewhere to go. Keep your plants moist, but not soggy. Check the amount of moisture every morning by sticking your finger into the top one inch of soil. If the soil feels dry, then give the plant a thorough watering. If the soil feels moist, then leave it alone. Lavender, rosemary, and sage like to dry out slightly more than other herbs.

FERTILIZER It takes food to make food! Your edibles will need plenty of their key nutrients including nitrogen, phosphorus, and potassium (NPK). These nutrients should be replenished slowly and continuously, because container-grown edibles deplete the soil as they grow. Use organic fertilizer such as fish emulsion, sea kelp, or worm castings to keep your plants looking green and robust. Make sure to slowly introduce the fertilizer into the soil. You want the plants to grow, but you do not want them to grow so quickly that they lose their flavor or aroma. Most container edibles should be fertilized once a month, tomatoes a little more often.

PLANTS SHOWN OPPOSITE: SAGE, ZUCCHINI, PEPPER

SOIL Use a good-quality organic potting soil for your herbs and vegetables, not standard topsoil. Organic potting soil is light, drains well, and usually contains a blend of peat moss, compost, perlite, sand, and topsoil. It's more expensive than other types of soil, but it's worth the extra cost, especially when you are growing edibles in containers.

AIR CIRCULATION AND TEMPERATURE To prevent mold and/or mildew from forming, edible plants need plenty of air circulation. As a general rule, most edibles prefer a temperature range between 50°F to 85°F. Avoid placing the plants next to an air-conditioning unit or heater. Placing the plants by an open window is ideal; the breeze can help pollinate some plants. (To give your plants some assistance with pollination, gently shake the stems every few days when the plant is in bloom.)

CONTAINERS Go big or go home definitely applies to the container size needed for most edible plants in the kitchen. Use containers that are at least six inches in diameter, but ideally eight inches in diameter. Most herbs and vegetable plugs are sold in four-inch containers. Always go up in size when you transplant. If you choose a six-inch container you will probably need to repot the plant in about three to six months. If you select a container that's eight inches or larger in diameter, the container size will likely suffice for a year or more. Tomato plants require containers that are at least twelve inches in diameter.

Use containers with a drain hole—don't rely on faux drainage. Your plants are going to need a lot of water and the water needs somewhere to go. Choose a container with adequate drain holes and use a saucer to catch any excess water.

CARE Most edible plants need regular pruning in order to maintain their natural, full shape. Herbs should be pruned and harvested just above a leaf node (the point on the stem where the leaves emerge) instead of directly off the stem. If you pull the leaves off without cutting the stem, you will end up with sparse, leggy plants. You can encourage bushy rather than leggy growth by cutting or pinching the stem two to three inches from its tips. Any flowers that form on herbs (such as on basil, cilantro, mint, and parsley) should be removed to delay the plant from going to seed. You may need to occasionally treat for pests or fungus. We recommend using neem oil; it's an indispensible organic treatment for most indoor plant pests and molds or mildews, and safe for use on your edibles (and your other houseplants).

PLANT SHOWN OPPOSITE: *CITROFORTUNELLA MICROCARPA*

THE MEDICINE CHEST

If you're interested in using plants for home cures, in addition to your home cooking, there's quite a list of plants you can grow. We love the idea of growing plants that have curative properties, and many medicinal plants can be grown indoors, so they are readily available when you need them. There are plants that aid the body's immunity and digestion, decrease stress and anxiety, calm sore throats and sunburns, and soothe insect bites and bruises. As with any plant that is ingested, be sure to check with your doctor before using them. Some of our favorite medicinal plants that grow well indoors include:

ALOE VERA Aloe is most commonly used to soothe burns. This plant grows from the center outward so you should use the outer, older leaves first. Break the leaf (you do not have to use an entire stem) and apply the sap against the damaged skin.

BASIL Yes, it's delicious in a sauce and smells great, but basil can also be applied topically to help heal minor cuts and scrapes.

CATNIP Besides being your feline's favorite treat, catnip can be used in tea and provides a great source of vitamin C. It can also be used to heal upset stomachs and mashed into a poultice to help heal bruises.

CHAMOMILE The dainty flower heads can be used as a tea to help relieve indigestion, anxiety, and sleeplessness. It can also be used topically to help relieve skin irritations.

ECHINACEA The leaves and roots can be used to make a tea. Echinacea aids in improving your immune system as well as providing some relief from colds and the flu.

GARLIC Garlic can lower your chance of heart disease, may protect against certain types of cancer, and provides antiviral and antibacterial agents that aid in fighting against the common cold and flu.

LAVENDER The scent alone has calming effects. The flowers can be used in tea to help treat insomnia, depression, and anxiety. Lavender oil has antiseptic properties that can be used to help clean minor cuts and bruises.

LEMON BALM The leaves can be used to make a tea or simply crushed and added to cold water. Lemon balm can help relieve anxiety and insomnia. When placed directly on the skin, it can help heal cold sores, insect bites, and minor scrapes and bruises.

PARSLEY A little pinch of parsley aids in fighting bad breath as well as flatulence.

PEPPERMINT The leaves can be used as a tea to aid digestion as well as soothe headaches. You can also crush the leaves and add them to cold water to help relieve nausea.

ROSEMARY One of the strongest and best-smelling herbs, rosemary is rich in antioxidants and vitamin A and can be used to help improve memory and concentration.

SAGE The leaves can be used in cooking or in a tea to aid with indigestion and healing ulcers. Sage can also aid in providing relief from menopause symptoms and as a mouthwash to treat coughs and sore throats.

THYME The leaves can be used in a tea to relieve indigestion or congestion. The leaves can also be crushed and used topically to treat insect bites, bee stings, and minor cuts and scrapes.

PLANT SHOWN OPPOSITE: *ALOE*

THE EDIBLE KITCHEN

Whether you're cooking at home or at a restaurant, nothing tastes better than fresh ingredients you have grown yourself. Our best advice to anyone who wants to integrate edibles into their indoor garden is to start slowly. Begin with a few herbs and then add a few vegetables. Once you have a good flow going between growing and harvesting, you can expand your ingredient repertoire. Below is a list of edibles that are well suited for growing indoors.

HERBS basil, bay laurel, caraway, catnip, chamomile, chives, curry, echinacea, feverfew, lavender, lemon balm, lemon verbena, mint, oregano, parsley, rosemary, sage, savory, tarragon, and thyme.

FRUITS AND VEGETABLES arugula, beans, beets, carrots, garlic, lettuce, onions, peppers, radishes, spinach, strawberries, Swiss chard, and tomatoes (cherry and mini varieties).

Keep in mind that certain plants work better when planted together than others. Below is a list of recommended companion plantings that work well for indoor edible plants.

PLANTS SHOWN OPPOSITE FROM LEFT: SAGE, ROSEMARY, MINT, OREGANO

PLANT	COMPANIONS
Beets	Garlic, Lettuce, Onions
Carrots	Beans, Chives, Lettuce, Onions, Peppers, Radishes, Rosemary, Sage, Tomatoes
Lettuce	Beets, Carrots, Chives, Garlic, Onions, Radishes, Strawberries
Peppers	Carrots, Onions, Tomatoes
Radishes	Beans, Carrots, Lettuce
Spinach	Strawberries
Strawberries	Beans, Lettuce, Onions, Spinach, Thyme
Swiss Chard	Beans, Onions
Tomatoes	Basil, Carrots, Chives, Onion, Parsley, Peppers

Note: Mint should not be planted with other plants because it will take over the pot.

When you're creating a mixed container garden, think about height, color, and texture. Place the taller plants at the back of the planter. These might include chives, lavender, lemon balm, rosemary, peppers, or tomatoes. Place any short or trailing plants at the front and sides of the container. These include creeping rosemary, lettuce, nasturtium, parsley, strawberries, or thyme. Think about placing contrasting colors or textures next to each other. The small, yellow leaves of a lemon thyme plant look great when paired against the black glossy leaves of purple basil. Possible combinations are basil, chives, lavender, peppers, rosemary, sage, and zucchini for full-sun and arugula, lemon balm, parsley, strawberries, and tarragon for part-sun.

PLANTS SHOWN: MIXED HERBS

LARGER BOUNTY

If you are interested in growing your own produce indoors, but want to grow something with more stature, citrus plants are an excellent option. With their beautiful glossy foliage, fragrant blooms, and minimal maintenance needs, citrus trees can make a wonderful houseplant. This large family of trees includes popular favorites such as orange, lemon, lime, and grapefruit. Some other less common but equally delicious citrus include yuzu, blood orange, and Buddha's hand citron.

Citrus trees like to dry out between waterings, and they appreciate sitting in your sunniest window or doorway. They thrive with four (or more) hours of strong direct sunlight, and bright light for the rest of the day. If you have a sunny outdoor space, these trees enjoy spending time outside during the warmer months, and being brought indoors once temperatures drop to around 40°F.

Citrus trees need to be planted in soil with adequate drainage. A very well-draining potting mix is ideal. You can let the top two inches of soil become very dry before each generous soak. If you start to see curling leaves, you've waited a little too long between waterings; curling leaves are a sign that your plant needs more water.

Another thing to consider with regard to indoor citrus plants is the container. Glazed ceramic and plastic pots retain more moisture than pots made with breathable materials such as terra cotta or unglazed ceramic. You'll want to adjust your watering accordingly, based on the rate at which the soil dries out. The container should also have a good planting depth. Citrus plants often get top heavy, and the extra depth will help stabilize the plant.

And last, but not least, you may need to assist your citrus tree with pollination. When you see flowers start to form, use a cotton swab to rub the anthers (the yellow pollen parts) until you see pollen on the swab. Then, gently rub the pollen onto the stigma (the slender filament in the center of the anthers). Repeat this process for several days.

PLANT SHOWN OPPOSITE: CITRUS TREE

THE UPCYCLED GARDEN

When you're thinking about planter options in your kitchen, try exploring materials from another era. Old lamps, old sinks, milk crates, and whiskey barrels can all be turned into vessels for plants. Antique or vintage tin cans are great for upcycling, giving the space a graphic punch of food-themed decor. Tin cans are often just the right size (six or eight inches high) and can be easily converted into a planter with the addition of a drain hole.

PLANTS SHOWN OPPOSITE FROM LEFT: BASIL, MINT, OREGANO, THYME, SAGE

UPCYCLED GARDEN

MATERIALS LIST

Hammer and a large nail (or a drill)

Tin can (with or without a lid)

Small rocks for drainage

Potting soil

Edible plant of your choice

STEP 1 Using a hammer and nail, or a drill, create drainage by punching 6 to 9 holes into the bottom of the can.

STEP 2 Place 1 to 2 inches of rocks in the can. The rocks will help prevent the holes from getting clogged with soil.

STEP 3 Fill the can about halfway with potting soil.

STEP 4 Take the plant out of its grower's pot and gently massage its roots. Place the plant in the can on top of the potting soil.

STEP 5 Surround the plant with more potting soil, patting the soil down firmly around the edges. The plant should sit about 1 inch below the rim of the container. You may need to adjust the amount of soil that you initially put into the tin to accomplish this. Make sure you do not bury the plant with soil above its original soil line.

STEP 6 Once the plant is snugly in its new pot, water it thoroughly (place the lid of the tin under the pot first). If your tin can did not come with a lid, you can use a plastic or ceramic saucer, or simply take the can to the sink when watering.

For more on how to care for this project, see page 209.

KITCHEN MAGICIAN

You might find yourself watering your potted plants more than you do your outside garden. This is a function of container gardening: Restricted roots need more water than plants in the ground because the plant's ability to reach for all available water is limited in a container. When they're growing in the ground, plants are often fed by groundwater in addition to rain. Given space to grow, the plant's roots will wick water from deep below the soil's surface. Self-watering containers follow the same idea: Using a wick to create a big "root" system, they are designed to bring water from the container's reservoir to the soil above. Self-watering containers are a great way to keep your plants healthy and allow you to go on trips without getting a plant-sitter.

Herbs and vegetables are great candidates for self-watering systems because they require a lot of water and a lot of sunlight. In normal container plantings, the nutrients get used up or washed away every time you water. With self-watering containers, the nutrients are recycled back into the soil via the water reservoir. This means less fertilizing is needed to maintain your nutrient-loving edible plants.

Choose edibles that will not overgrow the container, and start with compact plants that you can manage in your space. Options include basil, chives, lemon balm, lemon verbena, oregano, parsley, rosemary, sage, and thyme. You can easily purchase a self-watering container already packaged with everything you will need, or you can make one yourself with everyday household items. If you purchase a prepackaged self-watering container, be sure to water the plant normally until the roots establish themselves in the water chamber and begin using the self-watering system. Note that you will need to refill the reservoirs! Magic doesn't happen entirely on its own.

Of course, there is nothing better than making your own affordable self-watering container, seen opposite. Instructions for making one with a two-liter plastic bottle and an old sock follow on page 146.

PLANT SHOWN OPPOSITE: BASIL

SELF-WATERING CONTAINER

MATERIALS LIST

1 (2-liter) plastic bottle

Box cutter or scissors

Drill or hammer
and nail

T-shirt, sock, or felt

High-quality potting
soil (organic is ideal)

Starter plant (basil is a
good one to try)

STEP 1 Remove the label on the 2-liter bottle. You can do this by using very hot water and an abrasive sponge. Or, skip this step if you like the look of the label or plan to paint the bottle.

STEP 2 Using scissors or a box cutter, cut the bottle into two pieces, starting a little more than halfway down from the top. Snip off any rough edges so that both portions have smooth edges.

STEP 3 Using a drill or a hammer and nail, make at least 6 to 8 drainage holes in the top portion (the portion with the neck) of the bottle. They should be evenly spaced on all sides.

STEP 4 Using a T-shirt, sock, or felt, create the wicks by cutting two ½-inch-wide by 5-inch-long strips of fabric. Place the strips inside the top portion of the bottle (the half with the neck) so that the wicks trail out of the bottle's neck opening.

STEP 5 Fill the top portion of the bottle (the half with the neck) half full with potting soil.

STEP 6 Remove the plant from its grower's pot and gently massage the roots. Place the plant on top of the potting soil.

STEP 7 Fill in the sides of the plant with potting soil, making sure to press down firmly to eliminate any air pockets.

STEP 8 Fill the bottom half of the bottle with water.

STEP 9 Place the planted portion into the bottom half, making sure the wicks can reach the water.

For more on how to care for this project, see page 210.

WATERING BALLS

If you are going out of town and don't have a trustworthy plant sitter or a self-watering system, have no fear. There are many products that can water your plants while you're away. One popular solution is a plant globe. This is a glass sphere with a long nozzle, which is filled with water and inserted into the soil. When the soil is dry, the water inside the sphere slowly disperses through a small opening in the nozzle. When the soil is wet enough, the water will stay reserved in the sphere until more is needed. Depending on the size of the sphere and the water needs of the plant, this method can help you water for up to a couple of weeks (although one week is more typical). You can make something similar with wine bottles by poking holes in the cork or with soda bottles by poking holes in the caps.

Terrariums, or "gardens under glass," are a good choice for indoor gardens for several reasons. First, the plants are contained. You don't have to worry about your child or pet eating the plants or using them as toys. Second, this environment requires minimal care. You just have to figure out the right ratio of moisture and lighting for the plants to cohabitate. Third, they add a whole new dimension to indoor gardening. Terrariums can be designed to fit anyone's style. Colored rocks, sand, and glass create a colorful and quirky feel, while moss, bark, and soil suggest the completely natural and sublime. In essence, terrariums allow you to bring nature inside and remind you that on some level, we all live in climates that can be viewed on a macro or micro level.

VII: UNDERCOVER

TERRARIUMS PLAY A LARGE ROLE in blurring the boundaries between gardening, craft, and fine art. They are an object of display, precious and hidden behind glass and deserving of their own spotlight. Not only do they look great, but terrariums benefit plants by creating their own humid ecosystem.

CONTAINER There are many different plants and containers that can be used to create terrariums. The first thing you'll need to start your own terrarium is the vessel. The container should be glass or another clear material that allows light to pass through. Mason jars, apothecary jars, fish bowls, pharmacy jars, and cookie jars all work just fine. Keep in mind that containers with small openings may be more challenging to work with. Ideally, you want to select a vessel that is wide enough to allow your hand to pass in and out easily. Experienced terrarium makers may feel comfortable selecting a container with an opening just large enough to allow for the placement of soil and plants and a pair of long tweezers.

Vessels with lids, aka closed terrariums, are great for ferns, mosses, and plants that like humidity. Open terrariums are better suited for full-sun succulents, but can also house some plants that like low to medium light. For the most success with a terrarium, avoid mixing plants that have different care and living requirements.

DRAINAGE After selecting a container, you will need to create a drainage layer, because most terrariums do not have drain holes. To prevent plant roots from rotting, create a layer of faux drainage to separate the plant's roots from any accumulated water. Crushed river gravel or lava rock work great, but any small stones will do. The amount of drainage material to use will depend on the height of the container, but generally ranges from one to four inches.

CHARCOAL On top of the drainage layer, place a thin layer of activated charcoal. (Do not use the charcoal from your grill.) Activated charcoal can be purchased at most garden centers or aquatic stores. It will help keep the soil fresh and aid in hindering molds and bacteria from growing. You do not need to use a lot of charcoal; just a light dusting is fine. This step can be very messy, so open the bags with caution, and wear gloves or wash your hands after adding the charcoal.

SOIL The type of soil needed will depend on the type of plants you wish to grow. You can either use a traditional potting soil that holds water, or a succulent mix that drains more freely. Use enough soil so that you can create a hole in which to place the root-ball of the plant without disturbing the rock and charcoal layers below. For example, if you are adding a fern with a two-inch root-ball to a terrarium, then you will need to add at least two inches of soil to the container.

PLANTS SHOWN OPPOSITE: *AMARANTHUS*, REINDEER MOSS, FERN LEAVES

PLANTS It's best to select plants that share the same environmental needs for your terrarium. Ferns, mosses, and other assorted foliage prefer medium light and average moisture. Succulents work well together in high-light, low-moisture situations. Each plant has its own needs, so do a little research ahead of time so that they all play nicely together.

Keep in mind that all plants grow. You may eventually need to remove some of the plants from your terrarium if they become too large. You can also pinch back and prune certain plants to control their size. Ideally, you should select small specimens so that they have room to grow. If you plant too many plants, they may look great now, but over time the terrarium will become too crowded and need thinning out. Give each plant the appropriate spacing so that it has some airflow and room to expand.

PLANT PLACEMENT If possible, prune the plants before you put them in the terrarium. Remove any large leaves that might get in the way of the container or other plants. Remove any dead or yellow leaves. Also, thoroughly inspect the plants for pests. You want to make sure that you are not introducing any pests into your terrarium.

It's best to do a mock-up of your plant placement before you actually plant the terrarium. The largest specimens should be placed first. If the terrarium is viewable from all sides, place the largest plant in the center. If the terrarium is viewable from one side only, place the largest plant in the back. Next, add the smaller plants. Think about creating contrasting textures or colors when grouping plants together. Pair light colors with dark colors and large glossy leaves with finely textured foliage. Ground covers such as baby tears or moss should be added last.

DECORATIVE ELEMENTS There are many decorative elements that can be added to a terrarium to give it some extra pop or simply to make the terrarium more natural looking. Colored rocks, sand, and glass are great for adding color or textural interest to the top or middle of the soil. Bark, reindeer moss, or live moss can be added to the top of the soil to help hold in moisture and also provide a more natural-looking ground cover. Large minerals such as quartz, pyrite, or calcite can be placed in an open area of the soil and act as focal points of the terrarium. Remember, you are making a miniature landscape, so don't forget to have fun with it and add objects that reflect your personal style. These might include small plastic figurines, dried or preserved material, or decorative rocks and sand.

PLANTS SHOWN IN TERRARIUM: *ECHEVERIA, CRASSULA, EUPHORBIA*

TERRARIUM TYPE	LIGHT	WATER	HUMIDITY
Desert Terrarium	Full sun from a south- or west-facing exposure. At least 4 hours of direct sunlight per day.	Check for watering every 7 to 14 days. Only water the plants if the soil is dry 1 inch down or if you see signs of puckering or shriveled leaves on the plant.	Do not mist.
Woodland Terrarium	Bright, indirect light from a north- or east-facing exposure or at least 10 feet away from a west- or south-facing exposure.	Check for watering 1 to 2 times per week. Only water the plants if the top of the soil is dry or if you see signs of shriveled or dry leaves.	Mist every couple days. Note: Do not mist African violets, *Begonias*, or other foliage plants with fuzzy leaves.
Enclosed Terrarium	Bright, indirect light from a north- or east-facing exposure or at least 10 feet away from a west- or south-facing exposure.	Check for watering every 10 days. Only water the plants if the top of the soil is dry. Once you create the right balance of moisture, you should leave the terrarium closed. You may not need to water for months.	The enclosed container should naturally create humidity and have condensation that forms on the glass. If more than 25% of the glass is covered with condensation, remove the lid to allow some of the moisture to dissipate.
Aquatic Terrarium	Light varies according to plant type ranging from full sun from a south- or west-facing exposure to part sun.	Water needs to be changed weekly; algae should be cleaned off the glass. Keep water levels according to plant type (surface, submerged, or emergent).	High humidity will be maintained naturally in the aquarium.
Carnivorous Terrarium	Full sun from a south- or west-facing exposure. At least 4 hours of direct sunlight per day.	Check for watering twice a week. Plants like to be wet at all times. Use distilled water or rainwater.	Mist every couple days to keep the humidity level high.

PRUNING Remove any dead or dying foliage from the terrarium. Dead foliage can cause mold to form and the terrarium to rot. Because terrariums are living ecosystems, some plants will thrive, while others may fail. It's not uncommon, and most plants can be replaced fairly easily. Shriveled or brown leaves usually indicate a lack of water. Yellow or mushy leaves usually indicate too much water. Remove the dead or dying plant and its root-ball. Replace the plant with another plant with similar environmental needs and adjust your watering accordingly.

WATERING So, how much should you water your terrarium? This is one of the most important aspects of terrarium maintenance, and each terrarium has different needs, so there is no standard watering schedule. For general rule-of-thumb advice, see the table opposite. We recommend that you feel the soil near the base of each plant. If it's dry, give it enough water to moisten the entire root-ball of the plant. If it's wet, leave it alone. The amount of water varies depending on the size of the plant, but generally use a quarter of a cup for two-inch plants and half a cup for four-inch plants. For woodland terrariums, the soil should feel like a well-wrung-out sponge at all times. For desert terrariums, the soil should dry one inch down between waterings. Light brown soil usually indicates that the soil is dry, while dark brown soil indicates moisture. Never allow excess water to build up in the base of the container. Overwatering causes the terrarium to rot.

If your planting requires a high humidity level, misting the terrarium is beneficial. This is especially important for open-vessel woodland terrariums that contain ferns and mosses. You do not need to mist desert terrariums. Begonias, African violets, and other plants with fuzzy leaves should also not be misted because the water can damage their leaves. For closed vessels, 25 percent of the glass should have condensation on it. If you notice too much condensation forming on the glass, simply remove the lid and let the terrarium air out for a few days.

FERTILIZING Fertilizing requirements for terrariums are minimal because you don't want the plants to develop too quickly. Terrarium plants should be fertilized at most two to three times a year. This will give the plants the key nutrients they need, without causing them to outgrow their containers.

DESERT TERRARIUMS

Modern and minimalist, with an appearance straight out of a science-fiction movie, desert terrariums require a lot of light, an open container, and dry soil in order to thrive. If you want to use a closed container, moisture must be able to escape, so make sure the lid does not seal the opening completely. Desert terrariums use the desert landscape for inspiration and utilize cacti and succulent plants in numerous configurations. The design can be sparse and barren, featuring just one succulent and a bit of tumbleweed, or it can be full and flowerlike, brimming with numerous *Echeveria*, *Sedum*, and *Sempervivum*.

Some succulents look like marine plants and animals, which seems contradictory given their typically waterless living environment. *Crassula mucosa* looks like long and lean drifts of seaweed. *Crassula* 'Moonglow' twists like coral and has a phosphorescent glow. The flowers, shapes, and colors of these succulents mirror the sometimes otherworldly look of flora from a coral reef. Putting these plants into a terrarium gives you a mini replica of this underwater world.

When planning a desert terrarium, you'll first want to verify that you have adequate light. You will need full sun from an unobstructed south- or west-facing window. Then, you can then select the plants. Some succulents to consider are *Aloe*, cacti, *Crassula*, *Echeveria*, *Fenestraria*, *Gasteria*, *Haworthia*, *Kalanchoe*, *Lithops*, *Sedum*, *Sempervivum*, and *Senecio*. If not given enough light, the plants may start to look long and sparse. However, if you have part sun and are determined to create a desert terrarium, fear not. There are some succulent and succulent-like plants that can tolerate a little less light. These include *Aloe*, *Crassula*, *Cryptanthus*, *Haworthia*, *Rhipsalis*, and *Sansevieria*.

Succulent gardens are strikingly beautiful, low maintenance, and prolific. There's nothing easier and more gratifying than throwing a *Sempervivum* into a glass vessel and watching it multiply. We think that everyone should have at least one desert terrarium in their home, and instructions for making one are on page 160. What are you waiting for?

PLANTS SHOWN OPPOSITE: *SEDUM, ECHEVERIA, ALOE, HAWORTHIA*

MAKE
YOUR
OWN

DESERT TERRARIUM

Glass container
(8" to 12" in diameter
by 8" to 12" high)

Rocks for drainage
(lava rock or river
gravel are
recommended)

Activated charcoal

Succulent potting mix

2" succulents
(5 to 7 specimens with
different heights and
textures, such as cacti,
*Aloe, Echeveria,
Haworthia,* and *Sedum*)

Sand (optional)

Decorative material
(optional): colored
stones, preserved
moss, and figurines

STEP 1 Place 1 to 2 inches of rocks into the container.

STEP 2 Place a light dusting of charcoal on top of the rocks. (Charcoal can be messy. Apply a light spritz of water on it before you pour it into the glass container to help keep the mess in check.)

STEP 3 Place 2 to 3 inches of succulent potting soil on top of the charcoal.

STEP 4 Now you're ready to start designing! Before you commit to planting anything, set the plants into the container to see what configuration you like best.

STEP 5 Once you've settled on the placement of the plants, begin potting them. Place the largest plants in the container first. The exception to this would be if you were planting cacti, in which case you might want to place those last so that you can work without getting poked! Take each plant out of its plastic grower's pot. Do not massage the roots as you would normally with other types of plants. Succulents prefer their roots to be tight. Create a small hole in the soil where you would like the plant to go and place it into the hole. Fill in the sides with soil and press firmly around the base of the plant so that it is nice and snug. Don't worry if some parts of the succulent fall off while you are doing this. Succulents root easily and the pieces that fall into the soil may become new plants for your terrarium.

STEP 6 Repeat step 5 until all of your plants are potted. Ground cover or other low-growing plants should be planted last.

STEP 7 Now that everything is planted, you can either leave the soil exposed and consider the terrarium done, or you can cover the soil with rocks, sand, preserved moss, or any combination of the three. Consider black sand for a sleek, sci-fi look. White sand and desert sand have a modern, clean look. Preserved moss makes the terrarium feel more lush and gardenlike. Use shallow layers of top dressing so that it doesn't pile up next to the plants' bases.

STEP 8 Add in any special details. Quartz, agates, and other minerals evoke a mystical landscape. Miniature figures or animals make it more playful. These small details are what make your terrarium personal and can elevate it to an artistic level.

For more on how to care for this project, see page 210.

WOODLAND TERRARIUMS

Who wouldn't want a miniature forest growing in their living room? In an urban environment, woodland terrariums are the perfect reminder of nature. They usually feature a dense gathering of ferns and different varieties of moss and lichens. Woodland terrariums are the most natural-looking terrariums because they appear as if you just picked the plants from your backyard (if only you had a backyard!) and placed them in the terrarium. There is no denying the beautiful, lush green ambiance that these centerpieces provide, but before committing to a woodland wonderland, you'll want to make sure you can create the right conditions for it.

First, make sure the location where you want to place the terrarium has medium light. Think about the light at the forest-floor level. It is mostly indirect, perhaps with a few rays of soft, direct sun. This light can be simulated from a north- or east-facing window or ten or more feet away from a west- or south-facing window. Because woodland terrariums do not need direct light, they are a good opportunity to bring plants into rooms that do not get direct sun. Create a centerpiece for your dining table using one large terrarium, or cluster a trio of smaller terrariums together on the coffee table in your living room. As long as the room is bright with some natural light, your plants should be fine.

Besides lighting, you'll also want to pay attention to the moisture conditions of the room. Terrariums can be a great solution for a dry, indoor environment. If radiant heating is sucking all of the humidity out of your space, consider putting your plants into a glass vessel as a way to conserve moisture. The glass walls of the terrarium will foster water condensation, cycling moisture back into the soil while adding needed humidity to the plants and reducing the need to water them frequently. Don't forget to mist your woodland terrarium on a regular basis! You want to create that dewy, woodland realm vibe. Have you ever been to the Pacific Northwest? Now's your chance.

Possible plant options for woodland terrariums include *Adiantum raddianum, Asparagus plumosus, Epipremnum pinnatum, Ficus pumila, Fittonia, Hedera helix, Hypoestes, Nephrolepis cordifolia, Peperomia, Philodendron, Pilea depressa, Selaginella,* and *Soleirolia soleirolii.*

PLANTS SHOWN OPPOSITE: *ASPARAGUS PLUMOSUS, CRYPTANTHUS, PILEA, DRACAENA, ASPLENIUM*

ENCLOSED TERRARIUMS

Enclosed terrariums require little care. They provide plants with the perfect refuge from a cat who can take down a fern in five minutes flat. They also inhibit curious kids, resist temperature fluctuations, and keep plant pests at bay. Closed terrariums have a lid, which traps moisture inside the container. This type of terrarium is generally made for plants that thrive in humidity and like indirect, bright light. These plants include *Begonia*, different varieties of ferns, *Dracaena*, *Epipremnum pinnatum*, *Ficus pumila*, *Fittonia*, *Hedera helix*, *Hypoestes*, *Peperomia*, *Philodendron*, *Pilea*, *Selaginella* (and other mosses), *Saintpaulia*, *Schefflera*, and *Soleirolia soleirolii*.

Enclosed terrariums should be placed out of direct sunlight, so consider them for the center of a room or a bookshelf. Pairing them with preserved fauna adds an additional layer of complexity. Use the opportunity that an enclosed vessel provides to showcase your unusual fern species or that small bonsai you just picked up from the dollar store. Even a seemingly simple plant such as *Dracaena* or *Schefflera* can take on a mysterious aura if placed behind glass.

You can also use the benefits of an enclosed vessel to create the moss garden you've always wanted. Hair cap, rock cap, and cushion moss all perform well in enclosed terrariums. You can keep these simple and Zenlike with just a few clumps of moss placed in soil, or you can create a hill and valley landscape using bulkier pieces. Preserved moss such as reindeer moss can be sprinkled in to give the terrarium a more natural and textured appearance. It's really hard to go wrong stylistically with an enclosed moss terrarium. Everything looks beautiful and sublime.

Because an enclosed terrarium retains moisture and humidity, you really don't have to water your plants very often. The main concern for closed terrariums is too much water. Signs indicating the moisture level is too high include mildew or mold around the base layer or edges of the glass, yellowing plant leaves, or heavy condensation. If any of these occur, open up the terrarium and let it dry thoroughly before watering or enclosing it again. If your enclosed terrarium smells a little pungent or earthy when you open it, it should be fine. If it smells moldy and has mold growing in it, you should refresh the terrarium with new plants and soil. Once you find the right balance of moisture, you may not need to water for months. With the possibility of such a low-maintenance and visually intriguing terrarium, why not try one? Case "closed"!

PLANTS SHOWN OPPOSITE: *PEPEROMIA CAPERATA*, FERNS, *MASDEVALLIA*

PLANTS SHOWN FROM LEFT: *SOLEIROLIA SOLEIROLII,*
FERN, *PILEA CADIEREI, SELAGINELLA,* FERN

AQUATIC TERRARIUMS

The terrariums we've discussed need soil and at least some water (even if it's just in the form of humidity). There are also aquatic plant terrariums, or terrariums for plants that *only* need water. Some aquatic plants float gently on the water's surface, some grow entirely underwater, and some emerge from the water on smoothly arching stalks. These low-maintenance plants can grow in any very sunny window or, lacking that, with a powerful grow light in any spot in your home.

If you have a large vase, or a fish tank that's not being used, consider constructing an aquatic terrarium. For a naturalistic look, incorporate driftwood or stones. Soak the driftwood for a week before using it—otherwise your water will look like Earl Grey tea. (If the driftwood refuses to stay submerged, let it dry out and use it to mount epiphytic plants such as orchids, *Tillandsia*, and other bromeliads.) With an aquarium, you can create a naturalistic background above the water by using silicone to adhere cork or tree-fern panels (created from actual tree ferns) to mount additional plants.

There are generally three categories of aquatic plants: surface plants, submerged plants, and emergent plants that root in water and grow on or above the surface. Use a combination of all three for a varied display. Submerged and emergent plants will need soil media to root into. It is sold in many aquarium stores as a substrate for live-planted fish tanks. Your local aquarium store can also be a treasure trove of interesting options for a planted display—there are even bulbs you can plant underwater, often called "betta bulbs." Below are some aquatic terrarium plants to consider.

SURFACE PLANTS

EICHORNIA CRASSIPES (WATER HYACINTH) Large bulbous leaves that stand up from the surface of the water (high light)

HYDROCHARIS MORSUS-RANAE (FROGBIT) Round, smooth, nickel-size leaves (high light)

LEMNACEAE (DUCKWEED) Tiny green leaves (medium light)

PISTIA (WATER LETTUCE) Beautiful and slightly fuzzy green rosettes that bob on the surface of the water (high light)

SUBMERGED PLANTS

APONOGETON Grows from bulb, paddle-shaped leaves that grow up to the surface (medium-high light)

CRINUM THAIANUM (WATER ONION) Grows from bulb, very resilient, linear flat leaves (medium-high light)

NELUMBO NUCIFERA (LOTUS) Grows from bulb, arrowhead-shaped leaves that grow up to the surface (high light)

EMERGENT PLANT

CYPERUS PAPYRUS (high light)

Aquatic terrariums bring an entirely new dimension to the idea of terrariums. When you look through the glass, you are looking at a split-level world—one in the water and one out. The visual impact of these two environments is stunning. (And, your aquatic environment has the potential to house amphibians and fish, providing yet another dimension of entertainment.) This type of terrarium is geared toward anyone who wants a challenge and more distinctive look using plants that are not typically found in other terrariums. Aquatic terrariums need more maintenance— you'll need to change the water weekly and clean the algae off the glass, but the extra upkeep is worth the effort.

PLANTS SHOWN OPPOSITE: *PISTIA, LEMNACEAE, EICHORNIA CRASSIPES*

PLANTS SHOWN INCLUDE: *LEMNACEAE, TILLANDSIA, HARAELLA ODORATA, MUEHLENBECKIA AXILLARIS, CRYPTANTHUS*

CARNIVOROUS TERRARIUMS

If you've ever thought that houseplants can be a bit static or boring, consider a houseplant that can actually move. These are plants that can close their leaves at night (*Oxalis*) and when they're touched (*Mimosa pudica*), and even to catch live prey when it walks across an open leaf (*Dionaea muscipula*). In addition, there are houseplants that not only move, but are actively carnivorous. The term *carnivorous plant* can be used to describe the many species of plants that have evolved to turn live bugs into plant food. Some, like the famous *Dionaea muscipula* (Venus flytrap) are known for their lobed leaves that snap closed on unsuspecting insects, and others, such as *Drosera capensis* (Cape sundew plants), ensnare small bugs and fruit flies on their dewy, digestive-enzyme-coated leaves. Once dissolved, the nutrient-rich insects are a form of fertilizer for the plant. This adaptation developed in response to the poor soils of their native swamps. Venus flytraps and sundew plants require full sun in a south- or west-facing window, and their pots should always sit in a saucer full of distilled water.

With their distinctive shapes and their rich red and green hues (not to mention their ability to ensnare that pesky fly that somehow made its way into your kitchen), bog plants such as Venus flytraps and sundew plants make a great addition to your sunny windowsill or balcony. If you would like to keep your flytraps happy and healthy, don't trigger the traps. This will expend too much energy from the plant and it won't be able to grow.

Terrariums are the perfect housing for bog plants that need constant moisture, and making one is simple. You'll need a mixture of 50 percent peat moss and 50 percent sand for your planting medium. It is very important not to use potting soil, because it contains too many nutrients for the delicate roots of the carnivorous plants. Consider mixing different types of carnivorous plants together to create a nice arrangement with varying heights and different textures. Pitcher plants come in a range of colors, from bright red to chartreuse green, and provide an upright shape. Sundews and flytraps are generally lower to the ground and have soft delicate leaves. Any combination is stunning and will result in a Little Shop of Horrors theme. Don't worry about trying to feed your new friends. They are great at catching any little gnat or fly that comes their way. Just be sure to use filtered or distilled water to keep them hydrated, as regular tap water might have too many chemicals in it. If you have kids, put them in charge of the maintenance. They will delight in seeing little flies ensnarled in the traps.

PLANTS SHOWN OPPOSITE: *DIONAEA MUSCIPULA, NEPENTHES, SYNGONANTHUS* 'MIKADO'; BELOW: *DROSERA*

PRESERVED AND UNDERCOVER

A preserved terrarium is the complete opposite of the aquatic terrarium. This is an excellent route to go for people who dream of having a small patch of green tucked perfectly under a glass dome but who travel frequently and can only care for their plants between trips, or who live in a space that receives very little sunlight. For those individuals we say, "Don't lose hope!" Working with preserved plant materials, you can create astonishing little landscapes that need no care. Who says that plants have to be living to be lovely?

You can incorporate some of your favorite types of plants in preserved terrariums, especially dried versions of flowers that thrive outside but wouldn't stand a chance growing indoors. Think about using cut flowers, found pods and berries, and plant cuttings. Dry them hanging upside down so that they keep their upright form. They will most likely change in appearance, both in color and volume, during the drying process, but after they're dried, you can be selective about which material you want to use. Whether you dry your plants yourself or source some already preserved flora at a craft store or garden center, dried plants are a beautiful and affordable option for those who want the most hands-off but "plant-in" experience.

Once you've dried your favorite foliage, arrange it in the terrarium any way you like. Just avoid placing your preserved terrarium in a damp environment or in direct sunrays. By keeping the terrarium out of direct sunlight, you'll protect the plants' natural color from fading. If you introduce your dried flora to a super-moist environment, they might become damaged (they'll lose their preservation) or they might deteriorate from mold. This sounds alarming, but not to worry, a preserved terrarium is still one of the most effortless and economical styles of adding flora to your home.

Here's a list of wonderful foliage that preserves nicely:

Amaranthus	Globe Amaranth	Poppy Pods
Bachelor's Button	Grapevine	*Protea*
Bells of Ireland	*Hakea*	Queen Anne's Lace
Birch Bark	*Hydrangea*	Reindeer Moss
Brunia	Larkspur	*Scabiosa*
Cattail	Lavender	Scarlet and Blue Sage
Cockscomb	Milkweed	Statice
Craspedia	Mood Moss	Strawflower
Eucalyptus	Northern Sea Oats	Tallowberry
Everlasting Flower	Pampas Grass	Thistle
Fountain Grass	Pine Cones	Yarrow

PLANTS SHOWN OPPOSITE: DRIED *SCABIOSA*, *AMARANTHUS*, FERN, MOSS, FOUNTAIN GRASS, *GYPSOPHILA*

Preserved terrariums require no water, no light, and will maintain their appearance for as long as you keep them. When constructing your preserved terrarium, you don't have to follow the same steps that you would with a terrarium that features living plants, but we do have a few suggestions for making your terrarium look and feel established and beautiful.

First, emphasize different layers. Some of the best base layers include stones, rocks, gravel, sand, or soil. Remember, you're not going to water the terrarium so no drainage layer is necessary. If you use soil, remember that it's just acting as a base, like the stones or sand that you could also use. Next, create a green layer, or "positive space," on the floor of the container using preserved reindeer moss or other types of dried moss. You can break the moss apart easily and work it in with the base layer to create even more dramatic undulation in the landscape.

The final layer is where you will incorporate the preserved plant materials. Sometimes it takes some rearranging to get it to look the way you want. Don't be afraid to experiment with the materials you have. Whether the terrarium turns out full and lush, or minimal and simple, there's really no wrong way to go when the materials are preserved. You can create a landscape with dried elements that appear to be growing from the dried moss, or you can create a landscape that looks less natural. Try using contrasting colored sand in between the moss crevices, with the dried plant material popping through to create a striking contrast.

PLANTS SHOWN OPPOSITE: EVERLASTING FLOWER, TALLOWBERRY, *AMARANTHUS*, *PROTEA*

TERRARIUMS IN MULTIPLES

You can never have too much of a good thing. Such is the case with terrariums. With multiple terrariums, it's all about playing with height, shape, and repetition. Do you want your terrariums to stand on their own, or do you want them to appear like a cabinet of curiosities? Do you want the vessels to replicate each other, accentuating the positive and negative space found in each container, or exist as smaller specimens, in an array of repurposed bottles? Multiple terrariums offer an apothecary look when each planting is sequestered in its own vessel. Grouped together, they may appear to be a science lab experiment.

Any type of terrarium can be used in multiples: high or medium-low light, open or closed vessels. Apothecary jars, petri dishes, whisky bottles, flasks, and science beakers all provide good options for showcasing multiple terrariums.

Sometimes the place you intend to situate your terrarium can inform its theme. If an open cabinet with household objects such as toiletries is its destination, the terrariums can take on a medicinal feel. If the terrariums will be featured on a bar with liquor bottles, they may appear more specimen-like. Part of the delight of growing a plant is about marveling in the process of how it grows, its different stages, and how it changes visually over time. Multiple terrariums can celebrate these changes and highlight variations in leaf form, root structures, and overall shape by acting as a showcase for them.

If you are utilizing terrariums in a shelving area, be aware that the terrarium will not be viewed from all sides. Keep this in mind when you're selecting and planting. Place the taller plants in the background and ground covers in the foreground. You can further dramatize the variety of plants in the terrarium by manipulating the soil levels. This becomes very useful especially in situations where the terrariums might be above eye level. By exaggerating the soil levels you create the illusion of more depth in the terrarium and make them seem even larger than life. Now the only issue you'll have with multiple terrariums is where to put them all. Didn't we tell you? Terrariums are addicting.

Thank you for visiting the wonderful world of designing with indoor plants! Before you rush out and start buying plants that catch your attention, there are a few fundamentals you should familiarize yourself with in order to ensure a successful planting. By understanding some basic guidelines, novice gardeners will gain confidence to begin experimenting with indoor plant design, and the avid gardener may be challenged to try something new.

VIII: THE ROOTS

THE THREE MOST IMPORTANT FACTORS in caring for indoor plants are light (full sun, part sun, and low light); water (daily, weekly, and misting); and fertilizer (the dos and don'ts). Plants are living, breathing organisms, and like humans, they have different needs. It is advantageous to understand what those needs are in order to help your plants thrive. Once you understand what your plants' natural environment is, you can then do your best to mimic that environment indoors.

You also need to understand what type of plant parent you are, with regard to how much time you want to spend on caring for your plants. Are you a hands-on parent who wants to spend a lot of time cultivating your plants, or do you have a hands-off style? Being a good plant parent is really a matter of knowing yourself and your environment. Ask yourself, how often can or will I water my plants? How often do I travel? Think about what's realistic for your life, as well as your plants.

What is a houseplant? It may sound like a silly question, but not all plants will thrive indoors. Certain plants require a cooler winter sleep, or dormancy period, than what indoor climates provide. Often people ask if they can take a tree or shrub they see planted outside and move it indoors. More often than not, the answer is no, unless you have an unusual temperature situation. Outdoor plants need cool winter temperatures to induce dormancy, giving them a chance to rest and rebuild for the next season. An indoor plant generally prefers warm temperatures even during the winter, typically, from 60°F to 90°F. We understand the temptation to bring some plants inside—they are so lovely! But if you brought an outdoor tree—for example, a Japanese maple—indoors, it may last a few months or up to a year, but over time, it would begin to lose its leaves, and new growth would be inhibited, and it would slowly decline. If you've invested in plants to create your dream indoor garden, it's best to find ones that will thrive in indoor conditions.

Here are some exceptions to the rule. Some outdoor plants may be brought indoors for the winter, provided you meet their watering and lighting needs. Outdoor plants that tend to do the best when brought indoors include *Alternanthera*, *Alocasia*, *Begonia*, *Plectranthus*, *Coleus*, *Impatiens*, *Lantana*, *Passiflora*, and *Oxalis*. Larger trees and shrubs should be left outdoors unless they are a tropical variety, such as *Hibiscus*, *Gardenia*, or *Tibouchina*. After you've found a plant suited for indoor gardening, you will need to mimic its preferred light, amount of water, and type of soil in order to produce optimal health.

LIGHT

When selecting a plant, the most important consideration is its light needs. These range from full sun to low light, but what does that mean? How do you assess the light in your space? One way to describe full sun is to imagine a sunbather lying outside the shade of an umbrella in order to soak up the rays. Full sun, in gardening terms, means the sun's rays are directly hitting the plant. In the Northern Hemisphere, plants that need full sun should be placed in a south- or west-facing window where the afternoon sun is at its strongest and where they receive direct sun for at least three to four hours a day. Plants that prefer full sun include desert plants, some tropical plants, and most herbs.

Imagine a part-sun or medium-light exposure as a beachgoer who sits under an umbrella to avoid sunburn. Typical part-sun exposures are north- or east-facing windows that provide some direct light, but only at low-intensity periods of the day (early morning as opposed to afternoon). Some plants are described as needing bright, filtered light or indirect light. This means that the sun is not shining directly in a window, but through a filter such as frosted glass, a sheer curtain, or something that lessens the intensity of the light. Plants in this category are out on the beach, in the sun, but they've got some sunscreen on (most indoor plants fall into this category).

A low-light plant is not even at the beach. Low light is often typical when you live in a railroad apartment with space for plants only in a middle room or a bathroom, ten or more feet away from a window. Low light can also mean that there aren't any windows in the room and that you are using artificial light sources to mimic the sun. Many apartment dwellers, especially in urban areas, fall into this category. Low light is not ideal for most plants, but there are some plants that will tolerate it, provided you have enough artificial light to make up the difference.

In order to determine which plants will work best for you, assess your indoor environment to see what direction the light is coming from, if there is anything filtering or blocking the light, and how long the light lasts. A guide for determining which kind of light you have follows on page 184.

INDOOR PLANT LIGHT GUIDE	LOW LIGHT	PART SUN	FULL SUN
Room without windows / artificial light room	●		
North-facing window, 0–2 hours of sun	●	◐	
East-facing window, 0–2 hours of sun		◐	
West-facing window, 2+ hours of sun		◐	☼
South-facing window, 4+ hours sun			☼
Glass block or sheer curtain on a north- or east-facing window	●		
Glass block or sheer curtain on a south- or west-facing window		◐	

TROUBLESHOOTING LIGHTING

SIGNS THAT YOUR PLANT IS NOT RECEIVING ENOUGH LIGHT:

• Leaf color begins to fade.

• Plant stops growing or grows slower than usual.

• The length of the internodes (the space between leaf sets on a stem) increases and/or new leaf growth is smaller than usual. This is often referred to as "leggy growth."

• Stems and leaves lean toward the light (positive phototropism).

• Plant doesn't bloom.

SIGNS THAT YOUR PLANT IS RECEIVING TOO MUCH LIGHT:

• Leaf edges look burned or dry.

• Leaves appear faded or pale in places.

• The entire plant looks weak and droopy.

• Stems and leaves lean away from the light (negative phototropism).

PLANTS SHOWN OPPOSITE, CLOCKWISE FROM TOP LEFT: *PILEA, HOYA, CISSUS DISCOLOR, DRACAENA 'LIMELIGHT', TILLANDSIA, STAPELIA, AGAVE, ASPLENIUM, PEPEROMIA*

WATER

Watering is the most variable part of indoor plant care. Overwatering or underwatering is usually the number one reason indoor plants fail. We would love to give you a hard-and-fast guide to how often to water your plants, but because there are so many variables it is hard to be exact. Instead, the best advice we can give you is to feel the soil.

Some plants like to be kept evenly moist, which means you should water them when the soil surface begins to feel dry, while others can almost completely dry out before they need to be watered. Most plants fall in between those extremes. Consider a plant's natural habitat in order to gauge how much water to give it. For example, imagine a cactus's native environment—an arid desert, and how that plant has adapted to survive long stretches without water by collecting and storing water after very brief, intense, and infrequent periods of rain. To mimic that desert scenario, you will need to let the soil go completely dry, allowing the cactus to utilize the water in its "storage tank" until you water it again.

On the opposite end of the spectrum, imagine a plant that lives in a wooded, wetland forest where humidity and moisture are prevalent. This plant does not want its soil to dry out, and will need regular watering in order to keep its foliage looking its best. Generally, plants with soft, delicate leaves require more water than plants with thick, waxy leaves.

When you're watering a plant, you should completely saturate the root-ball rather than just watering the top layer of soil. This will ensure that all the roots are evenly moist. Apply enough water so that it runs out the bottom of the pot into the saucer. (If your plants are in pots that don't have saucers, move them into a sink or bathtub and water them there.) It is easier to maintain plants in containers with drainage holes and saucers, but if you are using a vessel without drainage, you can create faux drainage by placing a one-inch layer of gravel in the bottom of the pot. Excess water will collect in this improvised reservoir and help prevent your plant's roots from rotting. Be extra careful not to overwater, because, although this reservoir is a safeguard against rot, it is not fail-safe.

If you have a plant in a plastic grower's pot that you've placed inside another container without drain holes (called a cachepot), you should also be careful when you water; either remove the plant from its cachepot and allow it to drain in a sink or tub, or place a layer of gravel inside the cachepot to raise the plant out of any excess water, again to prevent rot.

PLANTS SHOWN OPPOSITE: *SYNGONANTHUS 'MIKADO', FERN, ASPLENIUM*

If the soil is consistently wet from too much water, your plant's roots will become deprived of oxygen. This gives the plant a droopy or wilted appearance, which people often mistake for needing more water, thus compounding the problem. A four-inch container requires approximately one cup of water; an eight-inch container requires approximately two cups of water, and so on. By following this rule of thumb, you'll encourage your plant's roots to grow deeply instead of shallowly, which helps the plant survive longer periods of time between watering. Light watering causes shallow root growth, so the plant dries out quickly and needs more frequent watering.

Plants that have been repotted into larger pots stay moist longer than plants in their original plastic nursery pots, requiring less care from you. We recommend you repot your plants sooner rather than later to provide more room for the plants to grow as well as to reduce their need for frequent watering. Other factors that affect how quickly a plant's soil dries out are its proximity to a heat source, indoor temperatures, how well established the plant is, soil type, and the material the plant's container is made from. Some of these factors change with the seasons. Generally, plants need more water in the summer, when they are more active, and less in the winter.

Use room-temperature water to avoid shocking or damaging the plant's roots. Filtered or distilled water is best for indoor houseplants. If you can store and use rainwater, you've hit the water jackpot. Letting tap water sit out for a day or two before using it will ensure a good temperature and will also allow potentially harmful chemicals to dissipate.

Try to be consistent with how much water you use and how often, and don't overcompensate for watering errors. When soil becomes excessively dry, it will shrink inward and pull away from the sides of the pot. If this happens, completely rehydrate the soil. Put the planted container in a sink or bathtub and submerge it under water until air bubbles stop appearing from the soil, then let the pot drain well. If you accidentally let a plant dry out, give it a good watering, but then get it back on schedule rather than continually soaking it.

TROUBLESHOOTING WATERING

SIGNS OF UNDERWATERING:

- Leaves droop.
- Leaves are crispy.
- Shriveled leaves fall off their stem or trunk. (Note: The plant may grow another set of leaves, so don't throw it out just yet.)

- Roots start to grow toward the surface of the soil.
- Aerial roots (roots that are above ground) may form (specifically on succulent plants).

SIGNS OF OVERWATERING:

- Leaves droop.
- Leaves turn brown and wilt. (These appear soft vs. crispy.)
- Leaves turn yellow (usually starting at the base of the plant).
- Leaves become mushy (a sign of root rot).
- Browning occurs on one side of the plant (a sign of root rot).
- Yellow and brown lines appear at the tip of leaves (often caused by "wet feet" where the roots have been sitting in water).
- New growth turns brown.
- Soil grows algae or mold.

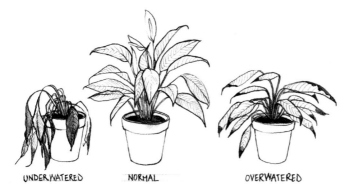

UNDERWATERED   NORMAL   OVERWATERED

On the following pages is a directory of common indoor plants with guidelines on how to select them based on the light conditions in your space and how often to check them for watering. (The more often you check to see if a plant needs water, the better.) Soon you will get into a rhythm with your new plant. Pay attention to seasonal changes that may impact its watering schedule. You'll notice that some plants can take a range of light and water.

Please note: This is a guide to how often you should check the plant for watering, not how often you should water. You will only need to water the plant if the soil feels dry. To determine if the soil is wet or dry, stick a finger in the soil about one inch down, or lift the pot and determine how heavy it is—you'll soon learn to judge how moist or dry the soil is for each of your plants by how much they weigh.

PLANT DIRECTORY

◐ Low light

◑ Part sun

☼ Full sun

💧 Keep lightly moist; check two or three times a week.

💧 Let top inch of soil dry; check once or twice a week.

◊ Let dry completely; check every one or two weeks.

Adiantum raddianum
Maiden hair fern

◑ 💧

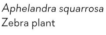

Anthurium spp.
Flamingo flower

◑ ◊

Aeschynanthus pulcher
Lipstick vine

☼ ◐ 💧

Aphelandra squarrosa
Zebra plant

◑ 💧

Aglaonema hyb. 'Siam'
Chinese evergreen

● ◑ ◊

Araucaria heterophylla
Norfolk pine

☼ ◑ 💧

Alocasia hyb. 'Regal Shields'
Elephant's ear

◑ 💧

Asparagus densiflorus 'Myersii'
Foxtail fern

◑ 💧

Aloe barbadensis
Medicinal aloe

☼ ◊

Aspidistra eliator 'Variegata'
Cast-iron plant

● ◑ ◊

Ananas comosus
Pineapple

☼ 💧

Asplenium dimorphum
× *difforme*
Austral gem fern

◑ 💧

Asplenium nidus
Bird's nest fern

Beaucarnea recurvata
Ponytail palm

Begonia rex
Rex begonia

Bromeliad aechmea
Urn plant

Calathea makoyana
Peacock plant

Calathea reseopicta
Peacock plant

Chamaedorea elegans
Parlor palm/neanthe bella
palm
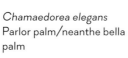

Chlorophytum comosum
Spider plant

Cissus rhombifolia
Grape ivy/oak leaf ivy

Citrus × Citrofortunella microcarpa
Calamondin Orange

Clivia miniata
Bush lily

Codiaeum variegatum var. pictum
Croton

Coffea arabica
Coffee plant

Cordyline fruticosa
Ti plant

Crassula ovata
Jade plant

Crossandra infundibuliformis
Firecracker flower

Cyathea arborea
Tree fern

Cyclamen persicum
Cyclamen

Cyperus papyrus
Papyrus

Davallia fejeensis
Rabbit's foot fern

Dionaea muscipula
Venus flytrap

Dracaena deremensis
'Janet Craig'
Corn plant

Dracaena deremensis
'Lemon-Lime'
Corn plant

Dracaena marginata
Dragon tree

Epipremnum pinnatum 'Neon'
Pothos vine

Euphorbia tirucalli
Pencil cactus

Ficus benghalensis 'Audrey'
Bengal fig

Ficus benjamina
Weeping fig

Ficus elastica
Rubber plant

Ficus lyrata
Fiddleleaf fig

Ficus microcarpa
'Green Island'
Green island fig

Ficus pumila
Creeping fig

Fittonia verschaffeltii
Nerve plant

Gardenia jasminoides
Gardenia

Gynura aurantiaca
Purple passion plant

Haworthia fasciata
Zebra aloe

Hedera helix
English ivy

Hemionitis arifolia
Heart leaf fern

Howea forsteriana
Thatch palm

Hoya spp.
Waxplant

Hypoestes phyllostachya
Polka-dot plant

Maranta leuconeura
Prayer plant

Mentha spp.
Mint

Monstera deliciosa
Mexican breadfruit

Muehlenbeckia axillaris
Wire vine

Nematanthus nervosus
(syn. *Hypocyrta nummularia*)
Goldfish plant

Nepenthes alata
Pitcher plant

Nephrolepis exaltata
'Bostoniensis'
Boston fern

Nephrolepis exaltata
'Lemon Button'
Lemon button fern

Nephthytis podophyllum
(syn. *Syngonium podophyllum*)
Arrowhead vine

Ocimum basilicum
Basil

Pachira aquatica
Money tree

Paphiopedilum hyb.
Lady slipper orchid

Peperomia spp.
Radiator plant

Phalaenopsis hyb.
Moth orchid

Philodendron cordatum
Vining philodendron

Philodendron selloum 'Hope'
Hope philodendron

Philodendron hyb. 'Congo'
Congo philodendron

Philodendron hyb. 'Moonlight'
Moonlight philodendron

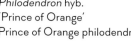

Philodendron hyb.
'Prince of Orange'
Prince of Orange philodendron

Pilea depressa
Creeping pilea

Pilea glauca
Blue Pilea

Pilea grandifolia
Moon valley plant

Platycerium bifurcatum
Staghorn fern

Plectranthus scutellarioides
(syn. *Solenostemon scutellarioides)*
Coleus

Sansevieria trifasciata
Snake plant

Polyscias fruticosa
Ming aralia

Schefflera actinophylla
Umbrella tree

Pteris cretica
Brake fern

Schlumbergera bridgesii
Christmas cactus

Rhapis excelsa
Lady palm

Selaginella spp.
Club moss

Rhipsalis pilocarpa
Mistletoe cactus

Senecio rowleyanus
String of beads

Rosmarinus officinalis
Rosemary

Setcreasea purpurea
Purple heart

Saintpaulia hyb.
African violet

Soleirolia soleirolii
Baby's tears

Salvia officinalis
Purple leaf sage

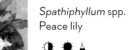

Spathiphyllum spp.
Peace lily

Stetsonia coryne
Argentine toothpick

Strelitzia nicolai
White bird of paradise

Thymus communis
Thyme

Tradescantia zebrina
Wandering jew

Trichilia emetica
Natal mahogany

Vriesea splendens
Flaming sword

Yucca elephantipes
Yucca

Zamioculcas zamiifolia
ZZ plant

PLANT SHOWN OPPOSITE: *PHALAENOPSIS*

HUMIDITY

A handheld spray bottle is a great tool in your plant-care arsenal. Your goal is to simulate your plant's native environment in order for it to flourish. For plants that thrive in high humidity environments, like a tropical rain forest, use a spritzer consistently. Establish a regular misting schedule. For plants that prosper in high humidity and direct sun, remember to spritz them when the sun is not hitting their leaves. Water droplets magnify the sun's rays, which can potentially burn a plant's leaves. To increase humidity without spraying the leaves of a plant, place a cup of water next to the plant. You can also place the plant in a saucer filled with water and pebbles and keep the water level below the pebbles. These methods are preferred for plants with very delicate leaves, like maidenhair ferns, or plants that prefer to keep their leaves dry, such as African violets or *Begonia*.

Misting has many benefits for indoor plants. In addition to increasing humidity, misting helps keep plant pests at bay. Many pests, such as spider mites, thrive in dry environments. Regular misting or even a humidifier will counteract a dry environment and help keep plant leaves soft and hydrated. Misting in the winter is especially important because radiators and other heat sources can dry the air and draw moisture out of plant leaves. Plants that thrive on humidity include *Anthurium*, ferns, *Fittonia*, orchids, most palms, *Philodendron*, and *Spathiphyllum*. Plants that prefer more arid conditions are *Beaucarnea recurvata*, *Chlorophytum*, cacti and succulents, *Epipremnum pinnatum*, *Sansevieria*, and *Yucca*.

SOIL

Using the right soil is important because it supports the health of your plants. Potting mix is not the type of soil that you will find in your backyard. Nor is outdoor soil generally used as a planting medium for your indoor plants. Most indoor potting mixes contain very little actual "soil." Depending on their moisture preferences, plants can require different soil types. General potting mixes might share a variety of ingredients such as peat, compost, sand, perlite, and composted bark, but will also be specific to different types of plants. For example, there are potting mixes specifically for succulents and cacti, and there are potting mixes for moisture-loving plants. Peat moss or coco peat is used to provide nutrients and increase moisture retention. Perlite is lightweight volcanic glass added to the mix to increase water retention and reduce soil compaction. It looks like small white styrofoam balls, or what people sometimes mistake for insect eggs. Decomposed mulch is also used to provide nutrients and aerate the soil.

PLANT SHOWN OPPOSITE: *ADIANTUM RADDIANUM*

Most indoor plants will take a regular potting soil. Succulents (including cacti), citrus plants, and palms generally prefer a fast-draining soil with higher amounts of sand or grit. Bonsais prefer a rocky mix with gravel and sand (they provide quick drainage). On the other end of the soil spectrum, *Saintpaulia* (African violets) prefer a heavy peat mix and highly absorbent soil, as do *Dionaea muscipula* (Venus fly traps). Keep in mind that most potting mixes have fertilizer added to them, so after repotting your plant you may not need to fertilize it for a few months.

Most garden centers offer a wide range of soil. Many people ask if they can just buy one bag of soil to use for several different types of plants. If you just need a little soil to top off a container, then most likely the answer is yes. Using a little bit of regular potting soil to pot succulents is not going to kill them. However, it is important to keep in mind that regular potting soil retains more moisture than potting soil tailored to succulents, so your watering habits should be adjusted accordingly. We recommend that you use the correct soil from the get-go rather than modifying your watering to fit the needs of a different soil type.

FERTILIZING

Plants need nutrients on a regular basis, just like humans. Plants require six key nutrients. The first three are carbon, hydrogen, and oxygen, which they get naturally from water and air. The other three are nitrogen, phosphorous, and potassium, which you'll need to provide. Nitrogen helps build the proteins that a plant needs for abundant foliage. Too much nitrogen may result in no flowering or fruiting because your plant is busy making new tissue (leaves). Phosphorous aids in root growth and helps the plant flower. Potassium helps with the overall strength of the plant. It aids in root development and helps build stress tolerance. Plants need other nutrients such as sulfur, magnesium, and calcium (in much smaller doses), which can be supplemented with organic fertilizers. Plants also need micronutrients, such as zinc and copper, which organic matter can provide.

We recommend using an organic fertilizer rather than an inorganic one. For the most part, organic fertilizers are not water-soluble and will release nutrients over time, reducing the risk of overfertilizing. It is easy to burn your plants by using inorganic fertilizers because all the nutrients go immediately to the plant in one large dose. It might look as if your plant has an instant growth boost, but the benefits are fleeting. In addition to feeding your plant an organic fertilizer, you should also add organic granular matter during the growing season spring through fall, which will not only feed the plant, but also the soil. This can be compost or a little fresh potting soil added to the top of your container. Just make sure you don't bury the plant in too much fresh soil.

When you scan the plethora of fertilizers on the market, you will see a three-number ratio on the label. The numbers refer to the ratio of nutrients—nitrogen (N); phosphorous (P); and Potassium (K)—in the fertilizer, always shown in that order (NPK). The numbers in the NPK ratio refer to the weight of each nutrient. For most houseplants a 5-5-5 ratio is generally acceptable. You might notice that some organic fertilizers will have lower numbers. This is because organic fertilizers can only report the nutrients that are immediately available in the fertilizer. The fertilizer will release more nutrients over time, so it is perfectly acceptable to use an organic fertilizer with lower numbers.

People often think they should feed their plants when they look sickly, but this is not necessarily the right response. If the plant has gone through a shock such as replanting, is fighting disease or a bug attack, or has suffered some other trauma, wait until it has recovered before you fertilize. Wait until the bug infestation has subsided or signs of healthy new growth appear. If you've repotted a plant, adjust its normal fertilization cycle because the shock of having been repotted and the fresh soil will reduce its need for fertilizer for a few months. When you repot your plants pay attention to the additives in the soil so that you know when to start fertilizing again. The labels on some potting soil bags will explain how long the soil provides nutrients, such as three months, six months, and so on.

Flowering and fruiting houseplants require more fertilizer, especially when they are in the active budding stage. Houseplants that do not bloom require less fertilizer. Many plants go dormant during the winter months, and during this period you shouldn't feed them. As a general rule of thumb, fertilize most indoor plants once a month from spring through fall and not at all during the winter months.

PRUNING

For some new plant parents, the idea of snipping off parts of your plant might seem unnatural and maybe even cruel. Rest assured, your plant will probably thank you for some selective pruning from time to time. There are a number of reasons to prune a plant, including keeping the plant healthy or shaping its foliage. No matter the reason, the same method of pruning should be used.

First, make sure you have clean and sterilized pruners or garden snips. Clean pruning tools ensure that you do not open the door for any diseases to infect the plant. Also, make sure that the pruners are sharp so that you can make clean cuts. We recommend using bypass pruners, which function like scissors. Always make the cut right above the nearest leaf node or branch collar, which is above the nearest intersection of leaves or branches. Proper pruning allows for the plant to heal itself more quickly, and also gives the plant a tidier appearance.

As a regular maintenance program, put a pruning check into your calendar once a year to assess how your plants are growing. The best time to do this is in late winter or very early spring, just before the plants start waking up again. Prune before you see signs of new growth (for example, swelling buds). Remove any dead branches or twigs, and thin interior branches as needed to allow more light and air to reach the center of the plant. By pruning back the longest branches, more energy will be sent to the rest of the plant, which will stimulate growth throughout. Exposing the plant's interior to more light will also promote a more dense, leafy growth habit.

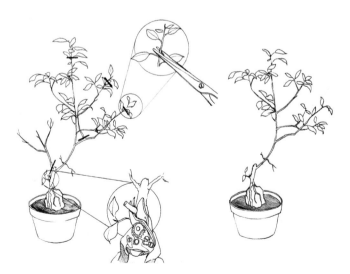

POTTING AND REPOTTING

Transplanting your plants from old containers to new ones can be scary for new plant parents, but don't worry, it's fairly easy to do. In addition to transplanting a plant from a plastic nursery container to a new, decorative container, there are a few other reasons for repotting plants. Below are some other examples that could indicate a plant has outgrown its existing pot and needs to be repotted:

• The plant's roots begin growing out the bottom or top of the pot.

• The plant seems top-heavy or unbalanced.

• The plant has a wilted appearance.

• The plant seems to need more frequent watering.

As a general rule, spring is the best time to repot plants, because that is when they are putting out the most new growth. Before you begin repotting, you'll need to know what type of plant you have so you can determine what type of soil best mimics its natural surroundings.

Next, measure the diameter of the plant's existing pot and select a new container that is about 25 percent larger. If the plant is in a four-inch container, the new container should be at least six inches across, if it's in a six-inch container use an eight-inch container, and so forth. As a general rule, you never want to use a pot that's smaller than the existing pot size, because you'll risk crowding the root system. However, if you use a pot that's too big, you risk drowning the roots, because a larger container will hold more moisture than the roots can handle. This often leads to root rot and plant death.

Another consideration is the drain hole, or lack thereof. It's easier to control the moisture level if the container has a drain hole, because you will be able to water the plant and see the excess water come out the bottom of the pot. This significantly lessens the chance of overwatering and root rot. If you select a container that does not have a drain hole, create drainage at the bottom of the pot by putting a layer (one to two inches in depth) of small rocks in the pot. The rocks will separate any excess water from the roots of the plant if you happen to pour too much water into the pot. Keep in mind that the faux drainage is a precaution, but it's not a guarantee—it's still possible to overwater your plant.

Now you are ready to transplant. Spread out some newspaper or towels in your work area because repotting can be messy. Remove the plant from its original pot, soil and all, by tapping sharply on the sides of the pot, and placing one hand over the soil around the plant's base, and inverting the pot. The plant should slide out of the existing pot. Don't pull the plant up by its stalk, because this can separate the plant's stalk from its roots. If the plant is rootbound and in a plastic grower's pot, you'll need to cut the plastic grower's pot down the sides to remove the plant. Keep the soil that the plant is potted in, unless there is something wrong with the soil itself. Loosen the existing root-ball by gently massaging the base of the plant until you see some of the roots start to detach from the soil. Imagine the roots are tangled strands of yarn. You are trying to create some open ends at the sides and base of the tangle. This will let the root system know it can move into larger surroundings. You might see that the root system has grown in circles—this is even more of a reason to get in there and loosen the roots up! Without doing so, the plant's roots may continue to grow in this way and not spread into their new environment.

Before adding new soil, place the plant in its new home to see how much soil you'll need to put in. The soil level in the container should be an inch or two below the lip of the pot so that when you water, the water won't flow over the container. If you need to add drainage material because the container has small drain holes or none at all, do that before you add the base soil. After the drainage and base soil have been added, place the plant in its new home and pack in new soil around the sides of the plant to fill in the extra space. Be sure to push the soil down gently around the sides of the pot and not leave any air pockets. Give it a slight dusting of soil on the top to fill in any soil that might have fallen through and another little pat down. You are now officially done repotting. Don't forget, most plants like to have a thorough watering after they have been repotted—it will help to settle the air pockets. The exceptions to this are cacti and succulents, which prefer to stay dry for a week or two and let their roots settle in without any water. Succulents and cacti can also go for longer periods of time without repotting because they like their roots to be tight and compact. It is also best to replant succulents and cacti when their original soil has dried considerably.

PLANT PESTS AND PROBLEMS

The first question that people always ask when they discover that a pest is attacking one of their plants is "Where did it come from?" to which there are a number of possible answers. Some pests can hitch a ride in from the outside on pets or clothing; some might sneak in through the window. They can surprise you at any turn. Most pests can be treated with insecticidal spray. Test a small patch of spray on your plant (move it away from direct sun first) before using a full application. If the small test patch results in discoloration of the leaf, you will want to investigate another type of insecticidal spray. When you reuse a pot from a previously infected plant, always clean it thoroughly with soap and hot water.

Below is a list of common houseplant pests and how to treat them.

APHIDS Translucent, soft-bodied insects about the size of a flea, aphids can multiply very quickly and are usually found in groups, sucking the juices out of a plant's stems, leaves, or flowers. They range in color, but are usually green, yellow, or red and are fairly easy to spot. Even if you don't see them, you will probably notice the sticky residue they leave behind.

Prune off any parts of the plant that are heavily infested, and then spray the foliage with a hose or by placing it in the shower and turning on the water. For more delicate plants, start with a more delicate stream as to not damage the plant. This will knock off most, if not all, of the aphids. Any that might be left behind can be taken care of with an insecticidal spray like neem oil, or simply a little castile dish soap mixed with water that can be applied with a spray bottle. Check the plant weekly to make sure the aphids are gone, and repeat the treatment if needed.

FUNGUS GNATS About the size of a fruit fly, fungus gnats will probably annoy you before harming your plant. Fungus gnat eggs, however, develop into whitish maggots that can cause damage to plant roots. They thrive in moist soil, and they are most noticeable when you're watering the plant because they crawl out and fly around. In a serious infestation, a plant will look sickly and possibly drop some leaves.

The easiest way to control fungus gnats is to let the plant's soil dry out more than usual between waterings, as the gnats need consistent moisture to survive. You can also make a trap out of a yellow sticky note with some petroleum jelly smeared on it. The gnats are attracted to the yellow color and will get stuck on the coated paper. If the problem persists, try using beneficial nematodes, available at most garden centers, which are microscopic worms that live in the soil and feed on the eggs of the fungus gnats. Some people find this idea a little off-putting because they are living creatures themselves, but the nematodes work very well, and usually take care of the problem after just one or two applications.

MEALYBUGS From a distance, a group of mealybugs look like fluffy white cotton. But upon closer inspection, the individuals look like some sort of prehistoric sea creature fossil with a long pointy tail. Like aphids, they suck out a plant's juices and can multiply fairly quickly. They are also very clever at hiding under leaves, in crevices, and other out-of-sight places, so examine the infected plant thoroughly in order to hunt them all down.

Thankfully, it's fairly easy to clean them off with a cotton swab dipped in rubbing alcohol. Afterward, apply a gentle spray of insecticidal soap—it should take care of any mealybugs that are still lurking. Check the plant weekly until you are sure they're gone and spray again if needed.

SCALE Scale is perhaps the strangest of all the houseplant pests. They attach their mouths to a leaf vein or a stem, and feed on the juices while growing a protective shell and reproducing, all from the same spot. They're usually brown, and the adults look like a flattened helmet and typically appear in groups.

It may take some time, but the best way to remove scale is by cleaning the plant with a soft cloth soaked with warm soapy water. A gentle spray of insecticidal soap can be used in conjunction with the cleaning-by-hand method. Check the plant weekly to make sure the bugs are gone and repeat the treatment if needed.

SPIDER MITES Technically not an insect, spider mites are more like actual spiders or ticks, building webs on the underside of leaves (usually) and forming large colonies very quickly. Prevent spider mites from taking hold by regularly misting your plants, as the pests thrive in dry conditions. This is especially important for ivy and croton plants, which seem to be some of the spider mites' favorite places to live.

If you discover spider mites on only a small part of the plant, prune the part off immediately, dispose of it in a sealed plastic bag, and treat the rest of the plant with insecticidal soap. Be diligent and check for more mites every few days. If they're covering more than half of the plant, set aside any sentimentality you feel about the plant and consider getting rid of it—the mites have probably already won.

FUNGI There are many infections that can appear on indoor plants, most of which are typically caused by high humidity, dampness, low light, or poor airflow. If you notice that your plant has a fungal infection, isolate the plant and begin treatment. One of the most common fungal infections is powdery mildew. It makes a plant look as if it has been coated in a light layer of white paint or chalk. Powdery mildew blocks a plant's ability to photosynthesize, and if left untreated, the plant will eventually die. The best way to combat it is to use an oil such as neem. Neem oil will smother the spores of the mildew, thus preventing it from reproducing. Heavily infected leaves should be pruned off and thrown away. Make sure you do not compost the infected leaves, as composting the leaves is not enough to kill the fungus.

Other types of fungal infections might take the form of leaf spots. These usually appear as dark brown spots surrounded by yellowish margins. They can also look like a series of small black dots. Sudden exposure to cold temperatures or overly humid conditions make plants more susceptible to leaf spots. It's best to prune off any heavily infected leaves, as they will not revert to being healthy again. Try to increase airflow in the room and lower the room's humidity. If the fungus continues after this first round of changes, use an oil such as neem oil to coat all of the leaves, making sure to also spray the undersides and the stems. Treatment should be continued weekly until the symptoms do not reappear.

Occasionally, the top layer of soil will grow mold. This is most common in plants that are potted in plastic pots because water cannot evaporate through the plastic. Moldy soil can also form when there is too much organic matter or fertilizer in the pot. If this happens, scoop away the top one inch of soil and replace it with fresh potting mix. You can also add powdered cinnamon or neem oil to the surface—they are both natural deterrents. To keep mold away from the soil, make sure your plant has adequate drainage. Plants should also be kept in a well-ventilated area. Any dead or dying foliage should be removed from the base of the plant. Wiping down plant leaves regularly with a dust rag or paper towel will also help keep mold at bay.

DESIGN ELEMENTS

PLANT PLACEMENT Choosing a location for a plant is a way of shaping your environment. Not only do you want to provide the plant with an ideal growing condition, but you also want to select a plant based on your needs as well. How much light does your space get? (See page 183 for how to determine your lighting.) Be sure your plant is suited to your lighting conditions in order for it to thrive. Is the plant directly under an air conditioner or heat source? How often are you willing to water the plant (once a day, once a week, once a month)? (See page 187 for more on watering.) Choose a plant whose watering needs fit your ability to take care of it. Consider the visual texture of the plant when you are making a selection. Do you want something light and airy such as a maidenhair fern for the center of a table, or do you need something more sculptural and stiff like a snake plant to stand out against a wall? The container and plant are an extension of your style. You should select a plant as if it were a friend. Whom do you want to hang out with all the time?

PLANT SCALE AND SHAPE Remember that your plant will mature. It might not even look the same after a couple of months, so keep in mind its future size when you view the plant for the first time. Ask yourself or someone more knowledgeable if the plant you're considering will change its current demeanor in a few months or a year. Will it suddenly bolt up and grow tall? Will it fall over and start to trail down the container, like a creeping fig? Find out how the plant will grow over time so that you can envision how the plant will eventually inhabit its container.

Do you want to accentuate the selected container's style? Choosing a plant that reiterates its container's form and shape is a design decision that potentially makes a more striking statement. Of course, you could also purposely pair the exact opposite together—we suggest that if you break the rules, break them all the way. Sometimes it just works.

Not only can the plant's form influence the container you choose, it can also impact where you place it. Is your newly planted construction going to live in the middle of a dining table? If so, it might be wise to use mid- to low-growing plants. You can leave the display on the table while dining and still be able to gaze over it at your dinner date or companions. If your new pairing is destined for a console tabletop with an open display shelf below, consider whether you want a trailing plant, as it may obstruct the view of the items on display.

PLANT TEXTURE The texture of a plant adds to the statement you want to make with your decor—it can help convey your style. Do you want your planting to express comfort and calm? Check out the delicate leaves of some of the members of the fern family; their soft forms exude a feeling of lushness and calmness. Or maybe you want to convey a strong, structured form by utilizing a hard-edged sculptural cactus? Let a plant's softness or edges speak to you.

PLANT COLOR When customers come into the store, they sometimes request a houseplant that blooms. We often ask why they want blossoms, and usually the answer is that they "want some color." Unfortunately, there are very few plants that bloom often enough to feel consistent, and many homes do not have enough light to encourage even a frequent floriferous display. For long-lasting color, consider the plant's leaves. Many houseplants are not pure green, but range widely among the color spectrum from shades of pink to yellow and beyond. You can set a tone with the color of a plant's foliage in the same way that you do with the color of a pot.

CARE OF PROJECTS

FOR MOUNTED STAGHORN FERN, PAGE 28 Staghorn ferns like to be in bright filtered light with no direct sun during the middle of the day. Typically, they like to be watered approximately once a week depending on how humid your home or office is. The sphagnum moss will retain moisture for the plant, but will also dry out thoroughly, creating a very natural habitat for the fern. Check the fern for moisture twice a week. To determine if your staghorn needs water, insert a finger in the middle of the sphagnum moss about an inch from the surface. If it is dry, then you should water the fern. To water the fern on the board, simply take down the board and submerge it in your sink or bathtub to resaturate the sphagnum moss. Let the board drip dry in the sink or bathtub before hanging it up again. Staghorns enjoy high humidity levels and benefit from misting on a regular basis. You should also fertilize your fern with general all-purpose fertilizer (page 200) during its growing season (March through October).

FOR MOSS WALL, PAGE 32 Preserved and dried materials need minimal upkeep. You may need to replace bits of moss if they turn brown or fall off. If *Tillandsias* are incorporated into the piece, you will need to mist them three to four times per week. Keep out of direct sun as the color may fade.

FOR MULTIPLE PLANTS, ONE CONTAINER, PAGE 58 Once the planting is complete, give it a thorough watering (see page 187 for more details on watering). Depending on the types of plants you've selected, check for watering one to three times per week. Place your plants in bright, indirect light or a little bit of morning sun (see page 183 for more info on sunlight). Over time, if your plants mature the way you imagined, then pat yourself on the back! If they grow differently than you had hoped, then make adjustments by pruning them or rearranging the plants in the container until a better configuration is found.

FOR MACRAMÉ HANGING PLANTS, PAGE 92 Make sure to place your new hanging plant in a spot with the appropriate lighting. The amount of water you give the plant depends on the type of plant it is. To test for dryness, insert a finger about one inch down into the soil. If the soil is moist, you do not need to water. If it is dry, water it. Because the container is clear glass, you'll be able to monitor the water level to make sure it never builds up at the base of the pot higher than the rock layer. As an alternative to a clear glass bowl, you can also use pots that have drain holes and saucers.

FOR KOKEDAMAS, PAGE 96 The kokedama requires regular misting—daily is best. Get to know the weight of your construction. If it seems exceptionally light or if the outer layer of moss feels dry, then you may need to soak it in a bowl of water for ten to fifteen minutes to rehydrate it. You can add a little bit of fertilizer to the water once a month during its active growing period (March through October) to provide some essential nutrients. Bright, indirect light is best.

FOR UPCYCLED GARDEN, PAGE 142 Most edible plants need full sun (at least four hours per day) and lightly moist soil in order to thrive. It's best to water deeply and less frequently than to water a little bit every day. We recommend that you fertilize your edibles monthly to keep them green and robust. See page 128 for more information on planting and maintaining healthy edible plants.

FOR SELF-WATERING CONTAINER, PAGE 146 Be sure to give your new, self-watering container plenty of light. You should also check the water reservoir weekly to ensure there is enough water in the base for the fabric wicks draw water from. Eventually, the roots of the plant will grow down into the base of the container, creating their own wick system. The only work you have to do now is to figure out how you're going to get more soda bottles without having to drink all that soda!

FOR DESERT TERRARIUM, PAGE 160 Desert terrariums require the least amount of maintenance, which makes them easily attainable even for the novice gardener. Because they contain plants found in the desert, these terrariums can go through a dry-out period of a week or more. We recommend checking for watering every seven to fourteen days. To determine if your terrarium needs water, feel the base of each plant. If it feels dry one inch down, then give it a small amount of water. You want to water enough to moisten the entire root-ball of the plant without allowing the water to collect at the base of the container. If you see bottom leaves start to shrivel or pucker up, it's usually a sign that the plants need more water. Yellow or mushy leaves are a sign that you're giving the terrarium too much water. Give your desert terrarium as much direct light as possible. A south- or west-facing window is best. Over time, your succulent planting may even reward you by sending up a flower stalk, which will further add to the alien nature of these plants and possibly blow your mind.

PLANT TYPES, FOR HUMANS!

Now that we've spent this chapter talking about what plants need, it's time to focus on you. What's your life like and what type of plant parent does your lifestyle allow you to be? Being a good plant parent is really a matter of knowing yourself and your environment. Are you green starved but crazy busy? We got you. Do you want to have a daily moment of Zen while tending to plants that need frequent TLC? We have just the thing! What follows are our suggestions for plants that best match your lifestyle as well as the light conditions in your space.

TYPE	PERSONALITY	HOME	COMMITMENT LEVEL	PLANT SOUL MATE
The Design Geek	You have an Eames chair.	Your house has tons of bright light and not a speck of dust.	You only want to deal with your plants on a weekly basis.	Air plants such as *Tillandsia*.
The Drama Queen	You go big or go home.	Your house has medium light.	You're okay with checking in on your plants a few times a week.	Large houseplants such as *Dizygotheca elegantissima* (False aralia) and *Dracaena marginata* (dragon tree).
The Earth Mother	You never forget a birthday.	Your house has tons of natural light or great morning light.	You can deal with high-maintenance plants and have time for regular mistings.	Ferns and mosses, such as *Platycerium* (staghorn fern) and *Selaginella* (mosses).
The French Manicure	You'd rather die than wear sweats in public.	Your house has bright light and lots of humidity.	You can deal with plants that need a thorough check-in every week.	Flowering plants such as *Paphiopedilum* (lady slipper orchid) or *Pelargonium* (scented geraniums).
The Jet Setter	You spend your weekends in your other house.	Your house has tons of bright light.	You want to set it and forget it.	Succulents, such as *Aloe* and *Crassula* (jade plant).
The Micromanager	You obsess over every detail.	Your house has low to medium light.	You can stick to a regular watering schedule.	Ground cover such as *Pilea depressa* and *Pilea glauca*.
The Serial Planter	You loved *Kill Bill* and *Little Shop of Horrors*.	Your house has tons of direct light or south- or west-facing windows.	You're fine with hand-feeding your plants.	Carnivorous plants, such as *Dionaea muscipula* (Venus flytraps) and *Sarracenia* (pitcher plants).
The Snow Bird	You travel at the drop of a hat.	Your house has low to medium to bright light.	You can check in on your plants twice a month, maybe.	Low-maintenance plants such as *Philodendron selloum* or *Sansevieria* (snake plant).

RESOURCES

For any of the projects or plants featured, please contact either Sprout Home location with questions.

Sprout Home Brooklyn
44 Grand Street
Brooklyn, NY 11249
718-388-4440

Sprout Home Chicago
745 N. Damen Avenue
Chicago, IL 60622
312-226-5950

SOURCES FOR DESIGN PROJECT INSPIRATION

Adam Gerard
ASA (asa-selection.com)
Ashware Studio (ash-ware.net)
Chive (chive.com)
Dalymade (dalymade.com)
DesignProject (designproject.net)
Gainey Ceramics (gaineyceramics.com)
Gold Leaf Design Group (goldleafdesigngroup.com)
Green Form (green-form.com)
Homart (homart.com)
Lechuza (lechuza.us)
Neo-Utility (neo-utility.com)
PAD Outdoor (padoutdoor.com)
Planterworx (planterworx.com)
Roost (roostco.com)
Tasi Masi (tasimasi.com)
Woolly Pocket (woollypocket.com)

CREDITS

Thank you to Alexander Rea and Nicole Miller; Alicia McCauley and Katie Hickman; Al Verik and Erika Schroeder; Angela Dimoff; Anna Macoboy and James Bowen; Aurora Ristorante; Billy Cotton; Bob Coscarelli and Karen Valentine; Britten Chroman; Brooklyn Winery; Celeste; Christer Cantrell and George Greene; Derek Love; DesignProject; Eric Staples; Humboldt House; Kings County Distillery; Lai-Chung Houlihan and Bobbi Houlihan; Liam Davy; Lisa and Michael Gabbay; Mike Madden; My Active Driveway; Natasha Liegel and Adam Newport-Berra; Nights and Weekends; Rashid Johnson, Sheree Hovsepian, and their son Julius Johnson; RJ Ciccaglione; Salvage One; Steven Piscione and Travis Ayer; Steven Teichelman; Teresa Surratt and David Hernandez; Thomas Calfa; Tiffany Francis; Tyler and Anna Love; and Wythe Hotel.

PHOTOGRAPHY Ramsay de Give, Maria Lawson

ILLUSTRATIONS Lai-Chung Houlihan

PROJECT CONTRIBUTORS Lai-Chung Houlihan, Stephen Hill, Natasha Liegel, Michael Madden, Greg Peterson

LINE JUGGLER Michelle Kamerath

STYLING Stephen Hill, Natasha Liegel, Anna Macoboy

STYLING ASSISTANTS Marlon Marcelle, Zach Ryalls, Allison Wall, Ellen Sparks, Sommer Tolan, Catherine Trudeau

ACKNOWLEDGMENTS

There are so many people who helped in the making of this book. Special thanks to our families, friends, and staff at Sprout Home. We would like to acknowledge Ramsay de Give and Maria Lawson for their amazing photography. The pictures could not have come to life without the beautiful styling work of Natasha Liegel, Anna Macoboy, and Stephen Hill. A HUGE thanks to Michelle Kamerath, whose line editing was invaluable. Additional editing and overall mental support by Dillon de Give and Michael Anderson. A big thanks to our agent Kari Stuart for introducing us to Ten Speed and our editor at Ten Speed Kelly Snowden, whose gentle, insightful guidance helped grow this book into its final form.

INDEX

Copyright © 2015 by The Sprout Home Company
Photographs copyright © 2015 by Ramsay de Give and Maria Lawson
Illustrations copyright © 2015 by Lai-Chung Houlihan

Published in the United States by Ten Speed Press, an imprint
of the Crown Publishing Group, a division of Random House LLC,
a Penguin Random House Company, New York.
www.crownpublishing.com
www.tenspeed.com

Ten Speed Press and the Ten Speed Press colophon are registered
trademarks of Random House LLC.

Library of Congress Cataloging-in-Publication Data

Heibel, Tara, author.
  Rooted in design : Sprout Home's guide to creative indoor planting / Tara
Heibel and Tassy de Give ; photography by Ramsay de Give and Maria
Lawson. — First edition.
      pages cm
  Other title: Sprout Home's guide to creative indoor planting
  Other title: Guide to creative indoor planting
  Includes index.
  ISBN 978-1-60774-697-3 (hardcover) — ISBN 978-1-60774-698-0
(ebook)
1. Indoor gardening. 2. House plants. I. Give, Tassy de, author. II. Title. III.
Title: Sprout Home's guide to creative indoor planting. IV. Title: Guide to
creative indoor planting.
  SB419.H398 2015
  635.9′65--dc23
  2014036284

Hardcover ISBN: 978-1-60774-697-3
eBook ISBN: 978-1-60774-698-0

Printed in China

Design by Ashley Lima

10 9 8 7 6 5 4 3 2 1

First Edition